PRAISE FOR
Awakening to the Truth of Who You Are

"Laurie Keene is one of the most inspiring and original teacher-thinkers we have today. Her unique way of laying out concepts (derived from her unique life experiences) creates a whole different reading experience in which the messages are not being read, but rather intuitively awakened from inside of you as if you've always known them. Reading this book, all I could think was—wow!! I wish I had it 20 years ago as a young man looking for a life recipe. Laurie Keene has managed to compose a clear and optimistic model for understanding our spiritual DNA. I truly feel that if this book were taught in schools as the fundamentals for creating a full life experience, the world would have a better chance."

—Yadin Kaplansky,
Psycho-Energetics and Brennan Healing Science Practitioner,
Teacher for Holistic Psychotherapy at Reidman International
College for Complementary and Integrative Medicine, Tel Aviv

"Laurie Keene is brilliant in guiding us through the Seven Phases of Human Consciousness and unifying all as we walk life's path. She has captured and articulated that divine part within all of us that seeks to learn, grow and remember who we truly are. A must read for anyone who knows they are in the midst of an awakening."

—Jeff Olsen,
Best-Selling Author, *Knowing, I Knew Their Hearts* and
Beyond Mile Marker 8

"Laurie Keene is possessed of a gentle yet powerful voice that wishes you well. Her book, *Awakening to the Truth of Who You Are* is the synthesis of a lifetime of heartful learning, and is steeped in experience (her own awakening story), knowledge (the result of a consistent and deep curiosity), and wisdom (the fruit of her profound intuition). Laurie's writing is as clear as spring water, and her gifts as a teacher and guide are alive on every page. She and her book are pure expressions of love. Do yourself a favor and journey with her. It may be the most beautiful journey you'll ever take. Bon Voyage."

—Cory Blake,
Co-author, *Overcoming Post Deployment Syndrome,*
Musician, Continuum Teacher, Integrative Health Coach

"A brilliantly written understanding of the process of spiritual awakening, *Awakening to The Truth of Who You Are,* clearly and gently guides you through the inner landscapes of your life. As you make this journey, Laurie offers tools that can assist you in anchoring your insights into your everyday life through what she calls, the living practice. If this book has found its way into your life, I would say to trust that the time is here for you to anchor your day to day life in the truth of who you are...enjoy the blessings of the way."

—Sherry Pae,
Spiritual Teacher, Artist, Nurse, Founder-Spirit of Ubuntu

AWAKENING TO
THE TRUTH OF WHO YOU ARE

Laurie A. Keene

Awakening To the Truth of Who You Are
Copyright © 2017 The Living Practice Press

The examples used from my work with clients are composites
with names and circumstances altered to protect identities.

All rights reserved. No part of this publication may be reproduced
or transmitted in any form or by any means electronic or mechanical,
including photocopy, recording, or any information storage and
retrieval system now known or to be invented, without permission
in writing from the author, except by a reviewer who wishes to quote
brief passages in connection with a review written for inclusion
in a magazine, newspaper, broadcast or online forum.

Library of Congress Cataloging-in-Publication Data
is on file with the Library of Congress.
LOC number: TXu 2-053-878

ISBN: 978-1-54800-177-3
Printed in the United States of America

Cover Photo: *Free* by JD Ardiansyah
Cover Concept: Deborah Black

Editorial development and creative design support by Ascent:
www.spreadyourfire.net

LaurieKeene   @LaurieAKeene
www.LaurieKeene.com

*This book is dedicated to
my students and clients,
whose courageous love
continues to teach and inspire me.*

*Brave souls all, they have dared
to reclaim the truth of who they are.*

*And to you, dear reader,
who have joined them.*

Contents

Foreword by Jeff Olsen 9

PART ONE: Opening the Door

An Invitation & Guide on How to Use This Book 15

1 / Being Human 23

2 / Introducing the Five Obstacles 49

3 / Obstacles and Why We Cling to Them 81

PART TWO: The Journey

4 / Introducing the Seven Phases
    of Human Consciousness 105

5 / Phase 1 — Sleepwalking 137

6 / Phase 2 — Denial 159

7 / Phase 3 — SOS (Help! Crisis!) 187

8 / Phase 4 — Knowledge and Resources 213

9 / Phase 5 — Opening 245

10 / Phase 6 — Committed 271

11 / Phase 7 — Illumination 309

PART THREE: Here You Are

12 / Consciously Co-Creating Your Life
     Through the Living Practice 335

Acknowledgements 360

About the Author 361

Foreword

We have vast and diverse experiences as what we call 'human beings' and it is imperative that we recognize our connection to one another and to the experience we call life. Although our experiences vary greatly, our emotions are universal. We all know the feelings of fear, joy, sorrow and love. Our universal emotions connect us, and it is our connection that is key to recognizing that we are far more than our human experience. We are divine eternal beings, in search of love and respect. Our paths may differ from each other, but our universal pursuit of learning unites us.

At the deepest core of our learning, is the lesson of love. Yes, to love those around us, but also to love ourselves on our own sacred path. Perhaps if we follow our paths with more kindness, together we can allow our souls to develop in such a way that begin to remember what we are here for and how to support each other along the way.

As we recognize and transform through what Ms. Keene calls "The Seven Phases of Human Consciousness," one will become far more connected with that part of themselves that is eternal and divine. In recognizing that divinity within ourselves, we may hope to mirror that divinity in everyone we meet. Each of us, dedicated to playing a key role in the life, learning, and support of the highest and greater good of the whole.

In exploring the pages of Ms. Keene's 'how to' masterpiece, these very complex ideas of oneness are articulated in such a way that we intuitively begin to see and live them. Transforming our selves from fear and judgment to love and acceptance. I am grateful Ms. Keene has taken the time to share what she has learned with the rest of us in such a way that we too can embrace our own inner power to overcome childhood trauma and negative thought patterns and transform them into wisdom and Light.

By following the principals set forth in this work, one can

navigate through life with more direction, peace, and joy. Ms. Keene expresses that we all have the power within us to create the life we choose to live. Her perspective outlined in these pages is that one can be at peace with their past, excited about their future, and grateful for the gift of free will.

–Jeff Olsen,
Best-Selling Author, *Knowing, I Knew Their Hearts* and *Beyond Mile Marker 80*

"It takes so much to be a full human being that there are very few who have the enlightenment, or the courage, to pay the price... One has to abandon altogether the search for security, and reach out to the risk of living with both arms. One has to embrace the world like a lover, and yet demand no easy return of love. One has to accept pain as a condition of existence. One has to court doubt and darkness as the cost of knowing. One needs a will stubborn in conflict, but apt always to total acceptance of every consequence of living and dying."

—MORRIS WEST,
The Shoes of the Fisherman

PART ONE
Opening the Door

An Invitation

Are you restless? Lost? Sad? Bored? Discouraged? Filled with worry or regrets?

Where are you going?

Are you searching for a purpose, a passion in life? Do you feel like you have "everything" and should feel happier than you do? Are you ill and isolated? Do you hate yourself? Are you afraid?

Where are you going?

Do you keep looking for the perfect mate, only to be disappointed when they fall short of your expectations? Do you feel misunderstood? Are you critical of yourself and others? Do you feel like you carry the suffering of the world?

Where are you going?

Are you impatient, easily angered? Do you find yourself complaining about your job, your body, your relationships, your finances? Do you keep trying to "quit" an addiction, only to find yourself going back for more? Do you walk away from a social encounter or the family dinner anxious and lonely?

Where are you going?

Whether you are hurting or struggling with these kinds of issues or you are already on a path of self-understanding, this book offers itself as a gentle guide and reminder that deep within you exists (no matter how inaccessible it may be right now) the essential truth about you.

THE TRUTH OF WHO YOU ARE

This truth is yours because it is you. It is simple. **The true center of your being is Pure Illuminated Consciousness.** As Pure Consciousness, you are limitless, infinite. Often referred to as the *Self* (you!) this Consciousness is *perceived as light, expressed as love, experienced as joy and peace.* This is the truth. It is yours.

It is mine. It belongs to everyone and everything, because it exists in everyone and everything. You never lost this truth—you just forgot it. I came to this understanding during the darkest time in my life. Through Grace I was lifted out of despair into the light of pure, loving Consciousness. I had let go of the mind-created world and I remembered! I will explain more about this in a later chapter, but for now let's just say that experience completely changed my life.

If the truth is as simple as I have stated, then why is it so difficult to grasp, experience, and live? Throughout history, spiritual seekers have sought to answer this question. This seeking has led to a burgeoning awareness of the truth, and for some, such as Buddha, Christ, Sri Ramana Maharshi, and Swami Muktananda, a complete return. Some call this return the state of being Awakened or Enlightened. I call it *Illumination,* because in this state, everything and everyone is revealed as *Light*.

So, how do *you* get there? The focus of this book is to act as a companion guide. It is designed to help you recover, remember, and return to the truth of who you are.

THE GUIDE TO THE BOOK

Our journey together is focused on three major areas.

1. **The Five Obstacles**: The first area of focus is to explore the Five Obstacles that stand between you and the truth of who you are. The obstacles are identified in Chapter 1 and introduced in greater depth in Chapter 2. Chapter 3 explores why we hold onto them and the process for dissolving them. In subsequent chapters, we will look at how your relationship to the obstacles changes and transforms as you move through the Seven Phases of Human Consciousness.

2. **The Seven Phases of Human Consciousness:** The second area of focus is in recognizing and understanding the Seven Phases of Consciousness that we as humans live. In pursuit of the truth of who we are, we naturally move and progress through these phases. We will identify the Seven Phases in Chapter 1 and introduce them further in Chapter 4. Chapters 5–11 are devoted to an in-depth exploration of each phase. This is to help you know where you are and where you are going.

3. **The Living Practice**: *Each day is an opportunity for you to apply and practice what you are learning.* The third area of focus is a section at the end of each chapter titled "The Key Points" (the main points of that chapter) and "The Living Practice" (composed of reflective questions, affirmations and inward journeys). You may want to record the inward journeys so that you can relax and listen to them when you are ready to take an inward journey. The Living Practice is an active process, designed to support your personal transformation and movement through the obstacles and phases. The principles of the Living Practice (explored in-depth in Chapter 12) are *creating, experiencing, pause, inquiry and transformation.* The Living Practice acknowledges that you are always co-creating your life. This is part of being human.

With greater awareness and dedication, the Living Practice helps you not only become aware of what you are creating and why, but ultimately it can teach you how to make conscious choices for positive, life-affirming creations.

This is done by deeply *experiencing* your creations (positive and negative), and while doing so engage in the process of *self-inquiry* (reflection, neutral curiosity and witnessing). Along with this is a practice called *pause* (slowing down so that you can feel what you are experiencing inside your body). This increases your ability to listen and hear your inner self.

It is through this continued process that you become self-aware. *Transformation* is a naturally occurring result.

For example, by being more aware of what you are creating, you will be able to experience what your creations *feel like inside of you.* You will learn how to sense when you feel good, centered, joyful, satisfied, or confused, troubled, unhappy with your creations. From there you will learn to utilize pause and inquiry to help you understand your intention beneath your creations, empowered to clear your intention when necessary.

The Living Practice helps you move from reactivity to responsiveness, from being closed to being open. As this practice becomes second nature to you, it awakens you, freeing you to consciously co-create your life.

Are you ready to return to the truth of who you are?
Let's begin our journey together, then.

1

BEING HUMAN

Our Gifts
Identifying the Five Obstacles and
Seven Phases of Human Consciousness

*"And suddenly you know:
It's time to start something new
and trust the magic of beginnings."*

—MEISTER ECKHART

Here you are, on your journey back to the illuminating truth of who you are. To begin, let's take the first step by looking at what it means for you to have been given a life as a human being.

BEING HUMAN: GIFT OR PUNISHMENT?

I have come to realize that being human is a gift. I didn't always feel this way. Having experienced tragedy, disappointment, illness, and loss like most humans, there were times when being alive was so hard. It felt unfair. Recalling the words from Burt Bacharach and Hal David's song *Alfie*, I would ask myself, "What's it all about?" I just didn't get the meaning of why I was here, why all of us were here and where I/we were going, especially when suffering. So, I know that sometimes being human doesn't feel like a gift. At times, it can feel more like a punishment, a sentence to be endured. But I can tell you that by taking this journey, you will be opened, just as I was, to the miracle and gift of a human life.

OUR GIFTS
We Are Co-Creators in The Living Practice of Being Human

We are here to learn, discern and *consciously* engage in co-creating our lives with Spirit. We are always creating. It's just that most of it is done unconsciously. By embracing life as gift, we can use the Living Practice to experience, pause, inquire and learn about our creations. In learning, we discern how to make healthy, loving choices for ourselves. And from these evolving places of awareness, we get to create some more! We get to develop in a way that, by remembering the truth of who we are, we can handle, grow, and choose love, *no matter* what happens in our lives. Transformation is like a flower. It naturally blooms within us as we do the work of consciously creating, experiencing, pausing and inquiring.

FREEWILL

Freewill is also one our gifts. Yep, that's right. We get to choose our path. We get to choose our creations. We get to choose to be open or closed. We can choose to grow or not. And from what I have been able to determine, the Divine, God, Spirit, never stops loving us, no matter what we choose.

I have also learned that when my freewill is aligned with divine will, it has always served my highest good.

SELF-RESPONSIBILITY

We are responsible for our choices. It's true. In fact, it is one of the consequences of having freewill. And while we are completely responsible for our choices, some events happen in each of our lives that we have no control over. What is within our power, no matter what, is our attitude. How we meet those events and whether we choose to close and react or open and respond, determines the course of our lives. When we welcome our choices and subsequently, our lives, as our responsibility, we are liberated and empowered.

OUR NATURAL GENEROSITY

One of the beautiful gifts in being human is our generous nature. When we learn something new and experience the delight of discovery, we want to share it! When we are in need and given something, whether it is a meal or an insight, we want to give to others in need. When we see someone in distress and reach out with kindness or a helping hand, we are opened by our own generosity. We are inspired by generosity, whether it comes from us or someone else. I have had the good fortune to become friends with a man named Joe. He lives on the streets in Philadelphia. It is obvious that he has been through tough times. He has the most beautiful, kind eyes. Over the years, I have given him food, clothing, blankets, and money. One time, I had a sack of coins and I gave them to him. The next week, when I drove into the city I saw Joe. I pulled my car over to see how he was doing. He came over to me and said, "Laurie, when I went through the coins you gave me I came across this old Liberty Head dime." He put it in my hand while saying, "I thought you would want it." I had been looking for that dime. It was one I had been given as a child. I was so happy that he had found it! Both Joe and I were expressing the natural generosity that lives in all of us.

Who comes to mind when you consider people who have inspired humanity? There are many I have admired, among them Mahatma Gandhi, Nelson Mandela, Helen Keller, Dr. Martin Luther King, President Lincoln, Jane Goodall, and Mattie Stepanek, a child whose optimism even in the face of death inspired with his poetry, such as the poem, *Future Reminiscing*:

"It is good to have a past that is pleasant to reflect on. Take care to create such a gift for your future."

It is those individuals who have generously reached out and touched us with their vision, integrity, courage, and love. As you do the work of remembering the truth of who you are, your own leadership will emerge and you, too, will quite naturally and generously share what you have learned along the way.

(Pause for a moment to consider: Remember a time when you extended your natural generosity to someone. What did you do? How does it feel inside your body as you recall that event? Remember a time when you were touched by someone's generosity. What do you feel as you recall this?)

CONNECTION AND LOVE

In 1994, when my mother was dying, my dad, brothers, sisters and I spent two days at home with her. She was in a coma. Curled up in bed with her, we read to her, sang to her, cried, laughed, and shared stories. My mom did not move during those two days. One hour before she died, my mother struggled to speak her final words. "I love you."

I wept as I listened to her voice. I knew that speaking those words took every bit of her energy. Her parting and most precious gift was to assure us that the most important thing in her life was loving us.

Our most precious gift is our instinctive inclination and ability to connect and love. When we feel connected (to ourselves and others), loved, and loving, everything is right "in our world." Even difficult situations are handled more easily knowing we are loved, and that "someone has our back." In the beginning, middle and end, loving is what matters.

We seek to connect, to belong. We seek to love and be loved. We feel isolated and separate when we are disconnected and unloved. So, we will find ways to fufill that longing, either positively or negatively. Negative expressions of connection and love may form through co-dependency, addiction and abusive relationships.

In my work (with individuals and groups), there is such a profound sense of homecoming when people take the risk to pursue their longing *to connect through love*. The risk being to drop defenses, become vulnerable and be authentic. This is the search for connection and love in its positive expression. Doing so opens the heart and connects one to the natural state of being the love that they are. I have often told my students and clients, "Almost more than anything, we long to open and reveal ourselves, both to ourselves and others, to be received and loved in return. We also long for others to open and reveal themselves, so that we can receive them and love them for all of who they are."

(Pause for a moment to consider—Do you feel connected or disconnected to yourself? Where do you feel connected in your life and to what or to whom? Where do you feel disconnected? While reflecting, what do you experience in your body? In your emotions?)

OUR CAPACITY FOR SELF-AWARENESS

One of the paradoxical gifts that we as humans have been given is a capacity for self-awareness. Its paradoxical nature is because while self-awareness is essential to realizing the truth within us, it can also get in the way of our realizing it. Essentially, self-awareness can support or suppress our search for the truth of who we are.

We need look no further than our animal friends to understand how we can use self-awareness to suppress the truth. Animals are present with *what is*. You won't find a cat or dog staring into a mirror taking stock of what they do or do not like about themselves. Humans, on the other hand, can look at a mirror and immediately judge and dismiss different parts of themselves. This is the kind of self-awareness that suppresses the truth.

When we use self-awareness to support our search for the truth, we cultivate this ability by going inside, reflecting, being quiet, inquiring, listening, becoming aware of our mind and how it thinks, feeling both the felt sense within our bodies and our emotional state. This is how we get to know ourselves deeply. A capacity for this kind of self-awareness is essential for moving through what I call the Five Obstacles.

> *"What you seek is seeking you."*
> —*Jalal al-din Rumi*

IDENTIFYING THE FIVE OBSTACLES

These are the obstacles that stand between you and the truth of who you are. They are an inescapable part of our human experience and conditioning.

THE FIVE OBSTACLES:

1. The Early Childhood Trauma and subsequent emotional pain you experienced. This is referred to as "The Wound."

2. The Negative Messages you received and the Negative Beliefs you formed as a result.

3. The Defense Systems you have created to protect yourself from being hurt or feeling the emotional pain inside you and the judging you do as part of defending.

4. Believing your Story is All There Is.

5. Believing your Thoughts.

IDENTIFYING THE SEVEN PHASES OF HUMAN CONSCIOUSNESS

As stated earlier, there are seven phases of human consciousness. Our relationship to them is not linear, nor do we move through them in a straight line. In other words, we can (and often do) move back and forth through them over the course of time. We might be in one phase in one area of our life and in another phase in other areas of our life. That said, when you have been on the path for a while, your consciousness begins to stabilize, affecting most areas of your life. When this has happened, the seeker lives predominantly in the Committed Phase.

The phases are listed here for you to get a sense of them. Which one do you feel like you predominantly live in? Again, they will be explored in depth in later chapters.

THE SEVEN PHASES:

1. Sleepwalking
2. Denial
3. SOS (CRISIS! HELP!)
4. Knowledge and Resources
5. Opening
6. Committed
7. Illumination

THE GOOD NEWS

From my experience, the Five Obstacles are part of humanity in its current stage of evolution. Every person experiences them. The good news is that they can be healed. Healing them is part of your life plan, your sacred journey. As you shift in relationship to them, you will realize these obstacles are no longer impenetrable. They become teachers, helping you learn the truth of who you are. As hard as it may seem in this moment, these *obstacles are your allies.* They hold keys to your self-discovery, understanding, and personal transformation. When embraced, your healing journey becomes a great adventure.

The beauty of the adventure is that once you have chosen it for yourself, *you will be on your way to loving yourself, living with an open heart, creating your long-held dreams, and realizing the truth of who you are.* Achieving this is the purpose of moving through the seven phases as you heal your relationship to the obstacles.

THE BAD DAYS

There will be moments when you will feel that this is anything but an adventure. There will be "bad" days, when the sun will simply not shine. There will be times when you may want to close this book, close your heart, and stop believing that your life will get better.

In these moments, I want you to say to yourself, *"No matter what, I will stay the course."* This is you activating your freewill for a positive choice. The Living Practice sections at the end of each chapter are written to help you develop your ability for inquiry and to connect to the truth inside you. They may also serve as comforting reminders during the "bad" days.

Like any worthy adventure, this path you are choosing calls for courage and perseverance. While infinitely rewarding, the path is arduous at times. I know. By the time I was twenty-seven, I was an old woman. Broken by years spent battling a life-threatening illness and witnessing a life that I had dreamed of slip away, I was lost. I lived, but I did not know why.

BOLD CHANGES

Then, just as the author Anais Nin wrote, "And the day came when the risk it took to remain tight inside a bud was more painful than the risk it took to blossom." After a final surgery, I decided that if I was going to live, I needed to live my life fully and to do so called for bold changes. I had lost myself and I needed to embark on the journey to find myself again. I left all familiar reference points behind—family, home, work, friends—and I ventured out, following only the voice inside me that said, "GO."

Two years later I was a very different me. I had begun to take the journey that I now know as the awakening journey to both the inner and outer worlds. In the outer world, my feet found their way hiking through the wilderness and deserts. My body healed in the sunny waters of the Adriatic. Turning inward and sitting in silence each day nourished my soul. What I discovered as I began to find my own rhythm is that my life just naturally slowed down. *It was in the slowing down that I could contact myself and feel.* I listened. I started to pay attention to what had been blocking my ability to love myself deeply and to what had essentially been killing me. I let loose the pain of my wound—the storms of rage, grief, and fear that had been held down in me for so long.

After the storms passed and the skies cleared, I realized the beautiful truth that had always lived inside me—the light, the love, the joy, and the peace—so simple and yet so profound. When we experience the truth, it ignites our passion for living. My passion for living continued to surface as I spent days with the herbs that grew wild on the hillsides where I walked and meditated. I brought my love of herbs into the kitchen, and for the next several years I focused my passion into cooking. I experienced pleasure as people delighted in the meals and desserts I prepared for them.

While my journey called for me to venture further afield in the world, the way for you is *uniquely yours*. You can come home to the truth while staying right where you live, if indeed that is what the clear inner voice within calls you to do.

WELCOME TO YOUR PATH—
A Sacred Journey and Great Adventure

I can think of no higher path than awakening to the truth of who you are and to all that is. It is a sacred journey, worthy of your devotion. It is a precious opportunity. It is liberating and fulfilling.

Together we will go through the steps to help you heal your misunderstandings, the obstacles that obscure your magnificence. Together, we will move through the different phases of consciousness. As you do this, you will begin to *experience the bright purpose of your life*. You will experience yourself more alive in each moment and open to the light, love, and peace that are your divine birthright. As you come to believe in yourself, you will realize that you are never alone. *Divine forces are always present*, guiding and loving you in every moment.

As you take the risk to pursue your dreams and learn to trust the way, you will be *surrounded by miracles*. Each time you find the courage to fully step into your longings and life, you will discover the outcome is greater than you could imagine. This is because you will have the elements of courage and passion aligned with divine will. You will find that you no longer need to measure up to others. Your striving will be only to meet and live from the truth you know to be you. This realization is within your grasp, and it is freeing.

During my years as a chef, I continued dedicating myself to learning and embodying the truth that exists within all of us. As I did this, Spirit led me from being a chef who puts the light in the food to being a spiritual teacher who helps people discover the light inside of them. Through perseverance, I have discovered my life's work, and it is infinitely fulfilling. As you discover the light within you, you will be led to your life's work, too.

BEFRIENDING THE OBSTACLES

The negative messages, beliefs, and habitual defenses are created out of fear. They suppress truth and deter love. Our work together is to help you arrive at the place within yourself where love befriends fear, thereby dissolving the misunderstandings you currently live by.

We will go step by step through the why and the how of your forgetting and unhappiness. From there, we will journey back onto your path of remembering.

Obstacles are just a part of the journey. Each person experiences them as part of the inheritance held within the darkness of our human misunderstanding. However, misunderstandings pass. What's eternal is the truth within you.

Besides the obstacles inherent in humanity, remember, we possess a natural generosity. One the many benefits to traveling this path is that you will create ways to bring the treasures you find in yourself back in to the rest of your life. In this way, you will be contributing to the evolution of human consciousness while experiencing the joy in giving.

> *"Don't ask yourself what the world needs,*
> *ask yourself what makes you*
> *come alive and then go do that.*
> *Because what the world needs is people*
> *who have come alive."* —Howard Thurman

BE PREPARED FOR MIRACLES

Do you want to feel at home within yourself, accepting and loving yourself just as you are? Do you want the courage to pursue your dreams, no matter how ridiculous they seem to others? Do you long for peace? Do you dream of having a sense of purpose and passion in your life? Do you want to be able to accept others as they are? Do you want to believe that you are never alone, that you are lovingly guided each step of the way? Do you long to experience life with wonder? Do you want to feel gratitude in the depths of your being for each breath you are given?

When you have come to understand the truth of who you are, these miraculous gifts and more will be revealed to you and in you.

LIFE WILL JUST KEEP GETTING BETTER

I have learned that the path never ends. What will change is your increased ability to be present in your life by utilizing the tools offered in this book.

Like the Beatles song "Getting Better" says, "It's getting better all the time." It does, it will. Stay the course. I have worked with thousands of people. I have had the privilege of witnessing their growth and joy as they have broken through barriers and dissolved the obstacles that kept them separated from their true selves.

Like every courageous explorer, you will need to persevere to reach the priceless treasure at the heart of your quest. Yes, you will need to cross oceans of misunderstandings, climb mountains of resistance, and confront the dragons of fear.

Then one day, who knows when, quite unexpectedly and miraculously through Grace, you will experience your heart filled with illuminating joy. Your eyes will be opened to the light and your very being will be the expression of love. You will feel the warmth of sunlight on your face as you receive the golden rays of Pure, Divine Consciousness.

In that moment, you may find yourself smiling, basking in the glow of your own inner light, at home in your inherent goodness, freed by embodying the truth of who you are.

CHAPTER #1

The Key Points to Our Gifts in Being Human

1. The Gifts of Being Human:
    a. We get to co-create our lives, consciously or unconsciously.
    b. We get to experience our creations.
    c. We get to utilize pause and inquiry regarding our creations and experiences to learn, discern, grow and transform.
    d. We have free will.
    e. We are responsible for our choices, not necessarily the events in our lives but our attitude toward those events.
    f. We have an instinctive inclination and ability to connect and love.
    g. We have a natural generosity.
    h. We have a capacity for self-awareness.
    i. We have the opportunity to awaken to the truth of who we are.
2. An adventurous spirit, courage, passion, and perseverance aligned with Divine Will are necessary for your journey.

3. You need to pause and slow down to connect with yourself: To feel, listen, and to follow the inner guiding voice of your soul.

4. Boldly step into your longings and life.

5. Experiencing the truth ignites your passion for living, and this will lead you to a sense of purpose.

6. You can learn to befriend the obstacles as you journey.

7. You can learn to consciously move through the phases.

8. You are never alone. Divine forces are always present.

9. Be prepared for miracles.

THE LIVING PRACTICE #1
Your Opening Ceremony

Creating, Experiencing, Pause, Inquiry, and Transformation

A Sacred Journey often begins with ceremony. The purpose of the ceremony is to honor the traveler, to wish him or her well, and to name the intention for taking the journey in the first place. Prayers, meaningful objects, or sayings help to energize the ceremony.

Create a small place in your home for an altar—*an altar that pays homage to your journey back to the truth of who you are.* Altars also act as anchors for the journey. They are a thoughtful reminder that the whole of your life is a sacred journey. Your altar can be as simple as making some space on a bookshelf or as elaborate as a small table chosen specifically for this purpose.

Choose objects for your altar to represent the truth of who you are:

1. One to signify the light within you.

2. One to radiate the love that is the expression of the truth that lives within you.

3. One that embodies peace and joy—the essential experience of the truth of who you are.

4. Two photos of yourself: one of you as a young child to remind you of the purity of your soul and a current one in recognition of you on your life path thus far.

5. Write or find a quote, affirmation, or poem that speaks to you during this time on your journey. Add this to your altar.

Remember, this is your ceremony and your altar. Give yourself time to discover the objects that are perfect for you.

Sit with the following inquiry and write about your reflections:

1. Why am I taking this journey?

2. What do I long to reclaim and heal within myself?

3. What do I want to create on my journey?

4. What are my emotions as I consider this path?

5. Pause. Feel inside your body. What do you notice? This is you, experiencing yourself as you go through the ceremony of gathering and placing sacred objects on your altar.

Complete your ceremony by allowing prayer or a stated intention to flow through you to whatever Source you connect with. You may call it God, the Universal Light, your Higher Power… Trust whatever words arise and know that they are affirming the journey you are about to begin. *Write it down* so that you may refer to it along the way. An example might be something like this: "Dear Divine Presence, I ask for courage and your loving wisdom to guide me as I take the journey home. No matter how long or winding it may be, I thank you for helping to guide me back to the truth of who I am. Thank you for believing in me."

After you have completed your ceremony, make a commitment to tend the altar you have created as you travel on your journey. Create space in your daily life to sit with your altar, to pause in quiet reflection and prayer. Feel free to add or take things away if your creative expression is called to do so.

An Affirmation to Support Your Journey

"Thank you, Divine Presence, for guiding me to this moment, where the adventurous return to the truth of who I am awaits me. Your belief in me and steadfast love assure me that all is divine order."

2

INTRODUCING THE FIVE OBSTACLES

"The wound is the place where the Light enters you."

—JALAL-AL-DIN RUMI

OBSTACLE #1: The Early Childhood Trauma and Wound

Every child lives through an event or events that are experienced as traumatic. The result of the trauma is an emotional wound the child then carries within them throughout their adult life. On a spiritual level, the purpose of the trauma and wound is to help direct the course of healing that the person/soul has come to do, what they need to heal to help them remember the truth that lives inside. On the human level, while traumas and wounds in and of themselves are not obstacles, the way that one typically relates to them *is* the obstacle. Second to that, they create the foundation for the subsequent obstacles.

FIVE DIFFERENT TYPES OF TRAUMAS AND WOUNDS

Wilhelm Reich, a psychoanalyst, and Dr. Alexander Lowen and Dr. John C. Pierrakos, both psychiatrists, originated a form of body-centered psychotherapy. Their psychotherapeutic model was based on their research that determined there are five specific childhood traumas and wounds that result in five defense patterns. Dr. Pierrakos further refined this model when he founded Core Energetics, also a body-centered psychotherapeutic approach. As a Core Energetic practitioner and former student of Dr. Pierrakos, I have experienced the confirmation of his findings with the thousands of people I have taught or supported therapeutically. While the classical Core Energetics interpretation of these traumas and wounds occurs chronologically from utero to four years of age, my experience has taught me that these wounds can occur up until puberty. Secondly, I believe all of us have experienced each of these wounds to a greater or lesser extent as part of our human experience.

In Core Energetics, the resulting defense systems are referred to as the Five Character Structures. It is important to point out that the names given to these character structures have no correlation with the psychological disorders that may appear similarly named. The outline of the traumas and wounds as listed below for each Character Structure are a compilation of a Core Energetics Training document prepared by Susan Thesenga and Alan Hill, Dr. Barbara Brennan's book *Hands of Light,* and my own notes as a Core Energetics student.

THE FIVE TRAUMAS AND WOUNDS ASSOCIATED WITH THE FIVE CHARACTER STRUCTURES:

1. The Schizoid Wounding

Trauma:

Hostile or rejecting/Mother/Caretaker/Environment

Direct Aggression

Occurs:

Before or at birth or early infancy: in utero, up to three months of age

Wound:

Not being wanted

Not wanting to be here

2. The Oral Wounding

Trauma:

Deprivation and abandonment

Occurs:

Breastfeeding period of early childhood: three months to one year of age

Wound:

Experience of abandonment and helplessness

3. The Masochist Wounding

Trauma:

Controlled force-feeding and evacuation

Humiliation about bodily processes

Invasion and control

Occurs:

Autonomy age: one to two years of age

Wound:

Shame and humiliation about self-expression

4. The Psychopathic Wounding

Trauma:

Seduction and betrayal

Being used

Occurs:

Early childhood: two to three years of age

Wound:

Self-perception as bad or inadequate

5. The Rigid Wounding

Trauma:

Rejection of sexuality and/or one's divine core essence

Occurs:

Genital age: three to four years of age or later at puberty

Wound:

Separation of love and sexuality

Inability to experience one's divine core essence

HOW THE TRAUMA CREATES THE WOUND

A trauma can be something simple, such as an infant not being allowed to suckle until sated, to a childhood illness, to the death of a parent, to intentional abuse. There is a broad spectrum to trauma. What is important to understand is that *each trauma is uniquely felt by the child/soul experiencing it*. Therefore, two children subject to the same event may have two very different experiences. For one it may be traumatic, and for the other it may not.

To illustrate how a trauma creates the emotional wound, let's look at one example. When I was five years old, I was diagnosed with acute appendicitis. I had emergency surgery and spent a week in the hospital. For five nights, my father slept beside my bed in a green leather chair. In the 1950s it was almost unheard of for the parent of a sick child to spend the night in the hospital. But my father insisted that he was not going to leave his baby girl. It was very reassuring to have him there. On the sixth night, my father was so tired that he told me he was going home to sleep. He gave me a slip of paper with our phone number. He told me that if I needed him, to give the nurse our phone number and he would come right back. I woke up in the middle of the night afraid. I told the nurse to call my father. I gave her our phone number, and she left the ward. She did not return. My father did not come. All night long I cried, terrified that my father was gone and that I was alone forever. Later, I learned that the nurse had never called my father. For me it was a very traumatic experience. I felt abandoned. At that age, abandonment felt like death. The wound that arose from that trauma was a fear of being abandoned and a feeling of helplessness, because even though I had our phone number, I was helpless in getting my father to return. Thus, the theme of abandonment and helplessness was something I focused on healing for quite a long time in my life. Another child/soul may have experienced that same event very differently.

Accepting the fact that you have an emotional wound and understanding it, sets the groundwork for exploring the spiritual purpose of your life. On the soul level, each person enters life with a healing plan. This plan is specifically designed. Each person has come to heal a misunderstanding that stands in the way of realizing the truth of who they are. From the soul's perspective, once a traumatic event occurs, an emotional wound is experienced and the soul's incarnational work has begun. My work has taught me that no matter what one has experienced, all life experiences, no matter how painful, hold the opportunity for healing. For me, part of what I came to heal is to know that I am never alone, and that the only one who can truly abandon me is myself.

OBSTACLE #2: The Negative Messages and Negative Beliefs

Negative messages are distorted and damaging communications meant to influence and control the recipient. They are formed out of bias and fear. They are often passed down from generation to generation without question.

The Negative Messages you have received, and in turn, believe, fall into three general categories:

Parental Messages: The messages you have received from your parents or guardians (whether intended or not).

Societal Messages: The messages you have received from society. These can be looked at from the religious, political, racial, gender, economical, and/or cultural perspective.

Self-Generated Messages: The messages you tell yourself (whether conscious or not).

Let's look at each of the three categories to get a sense of how a negative message can be generated. One potent negative message I received was about my body image. I have worked with many people who have struggled with the same message. I am going to use that as our example here, as it is one that can easily come from all three messaging sources.

Parental Messages: When I entered pre-puberty at age ten, my angular body began to change. I got rounder. I put on weight. I was also taller than most girls my age. My father talked to me about my weight and suggested I go on a diet. Over the years, the message I heard (whether intended by my father or not) was that love and approval are based on physical appearance. It all depends on size and weight.

Societal Messages: Open a magazine, turn on the TV, go to the movies and get the same message about attractiveness, value, and weight. Both women and men are given the message that to be desired and be of value they need to be thin. When I was in my late teens, I considered modeling. I am almost six feet tall and at the time I weighed 126 pounds. The agency that had an interest in representing me told me that I needed to lose at least five more pounds to be perfect. As I listened to them I felt sick. I was already a size two and unwell from being underweight.

Messages We Tell Ourselves: These messages are often residuals of the parental and societal messages. The individual typically internalizes those messages as if they are their own. For me, I became ashamed of my body. I also feared and dis-trusted my body. Food had become my enemy. I hated myself whenever I put on weight and I liked myself when I lost it. I became bulimic for a few years in an attempt to control my ever-changing form. For many years, I based my femininity, attractiveness, and overall self-worth on my weight and dress size.

The Negative Beliefs you have formed about yourself are a result of your wound and the negative messages.

While the issue of weight, attractiveness, and value is pandemic, there are a multitude of negative messages such as:

"You are worth nothing" from an abusive partner or parent

"You are slow and stupid" from a teacher or parent

"You are guilty, your soul is dark, and you need to pray for redemption" from a religion

"You are a deviant if you are homosexual" from family, friends, society, religion

"You don't have value unless you have a profession your parents and family approve of" from parents or society

"You are untrustworthy if you are from a different culture or race" from society

"You are unlovable" from a partner or family

"You are selfish" from a sibling

"You are different or weird" from a group of bullies

"You are not loyal if you have a different opinion or view" from your family or peers

All negative messages boil down to *one universal belief* that is held within humanity: *There is something wrong with you.* Therefore, you believe, *I must be bad.*

Essentially, *negative beliefs are erroneous conclusions about yourself and life.* They are misunderstandings. Whether developed from a message or the wound, these beliefs stand in the way of you and the truth of who you are.

An example of a negative belief comes from a client of mine in her mid-forties, a talented artist. In one session, she shared that she only felt worthy if she lived the life her parents thought was important. A worthy life to them did not include her being an artist. She had spent most of her life trying to conform to her parent's wishes. As a result, she had been very unhappy. Eventually, her unhappiness outweighed the pain of disappointing her parents. She began taking oil painting classes. Her work received wonderful reviews. She now earns her living doing what she loves—painting. Despite this, she still has moments when she *believes* she is selfish and guilty for following her own dreams.

OBSTACLE #3: The Defense Systems you created to protect yourself from being hurt or feeling the pain of the emotional wound and the judging that holds the defense systems in place.

The purpose of defending is to protect yourself from whatever or whomever you perceive as a threat to your life and/or wellbeing. *All living organisms have defense systems to sustain life.* Therefore, defense systems have their healthy and rightful place. These defenses are *an automatic energetic reaction* against what or who is perceived as a threat. A porcupine will raise its spiny needles; a skunk will spray its odoriferous scent. Humans have many different types of defenses. For example, one person may try to shrink away, pretending to be invisible, while another may puff up their shoulders and raise their fists.

(Pause for a moment to consider: How do you automatically react/defend when you feel threatened? What does this feel like inside your body? What does your energetic defense look like? Take a moment to draw it.)

The trauma, wounds, and messages that we received as

young children were *experienced* as imminent threats. In reaction, the child "survived" by instinctively and unconsciously *defending against the pain* of these events by withdrawing, aggressing, shutting down, and so on. This is also referred to as *flight, fight, or freeze*. This is done as a natural means of survival. The traumatic experience is too much for the child to process and assimilate at such a young age, and thus a defense is used to preserve a sense of self.

(Pause for a moment to consider: Now that you have drawn your energetic defense, which is it most like—flight, fight or freeze?)

Defending against the pain creates a separation (between the event and the emotional pain) within the child. This separation/split lays the groundwork for healing in one's life as the adult progresses through the seven phases. For some children, the trauma was indeed a direct threat of life. For others like myself, my father not returning to the hospital was not life threatening. As a five-year-old, however, I experienced it as such. No matter the degree of your trauma and wound, in the words of a former therapist, "All emotional wounds are third-degree burns."

Unfortunately, over time defense systems end up being used like the boy who cried wolf in the children's story. *They are used when not really needed. They become habitual.* Habitual to the point that most of us react and defend against people and events throughout our day. Our habitual defense becomes activated when anything that *feels like a threat to our sense of self is experienced, or, when the pain of our wound is ignited.* We not only employ our energetic defenses; we may also act on them with words, thoughts, and feelings.

Here are a few examples where someone might be using their defenses habitually:

*The car in the lane next to you signals that they are moving into your lane ahead of you. You automatically speed up so they can't.

*A group of friends decides to meet for dinner and you are not invited. The next time one of them calls, you don't answer.

*The person in front of you at the checkout line is moving slowly. You are already late for an appointment. You start pushing your cart forward, to 'tell' the person to 'get moving.'

*Your boyfriend or girlfriend breaks up with you. You automatically think you did something wrong to "make them leave" and you grab food, alcohol, anything to defend against feeling. Alternatively, you start talking about how awful they are and everything they did wrong.

*(Pause for a moment to consider:
Are any of the above examples familiar?
Where in your life do habitually defend? Why?
How many times a day do you typically defend?
You may want to spend one day counting them.
You might surprise yourself.)*

Our habitual defenses are endless. They are the result of unresolved traumas, wounds, messages, and belief systems. *We defend so we don't have to feel the original pain.* In his book *Core Energetics,* Dr. Pierrakos called this "patterns of denial." The result is that defenses end up creating a lot of secondary pain. The original pain, when suppressed by defending, prevents us from experiencing the truth of who we are.

JUDGING

I call judging the Great Separator. Judging is as automatic as our energetic defense systems. Our rapid-fire thinking approves or disapproves of just about everyone and everything. It keeps us separate. We quickly make assumptions and then draw conclusions about situations, events, and people (ourselves and others) to defend against being present, open, and in the unknown. Judging is the cement of our defense systems. Often, our judging leads to a demand that either the other or the self must be or do something different to allay negative judging. In my experience, *all demands toward the self or other are acts of violence.*

> *"Watch how your mind judges. Judgment comes, in part, out of your own fear. You judge other people because you're not comfortable in your own being... the judging mind is very divisive. It keeps us separate. Separation closes your heart." —Ram Dass*

OBSTACLE #4: Believing Your Story Is All There Is

Stories and the art of storytelling can be a very powerful tool for teaching and relaying history and traditional wisdom. Many indigenous cultures use oral storytelling as a way of keeping records. Jesus taught in parables. I am not referring to those kinds of stories as obstacles, though they have the potential to be if the story is colored by limiting cultural beliefs and distorted perceptions.

For our purposes, I am speaking about the two kinds of personal stories that stand in the way of the truth of who we are. The first story is our perceptional recall and emotional experiences of our own history. It holds the gathered memories and imprints of our lives. The second kind of story is the type we make up every day about ourselves, events, life, and others.

While recalling life's events can be useful on many levels, we tend to believe that our story is the epitome of reality. We then *give our stories the power to identify life and us*. This is not only limiting; it is misleading.

A client of mine experienced one cruelty after another in her early life. She had been raised in a family where the threat of violence was always present. She was born right before the Second World War and was the oldest of several children. Her mother was mentally ill and prone to violent behavior toward my client. While her siblings could go outside and play, my client was forced to do the chores that running a house demanded. She was not allowed to speak to the neighbors. She was not allowed to voice her opinion or to speak of things that interested her. If she needed something, the answer was always no. Once, she was terribly injured and had to spend several weeks in a hospital. Her mother never visited her. She carried a lot of grief about her childhood and felt deeply that there was something wrong with her for having been treated so badly. She left home at eighteen, although her parents told her she was supposed to take care of them. Out on her own, she had a few relationships—all of them with women. In each relationship, she felt that she was the victim and that sooner or later she would end up being treated badly. Therefore, she had chosen celibacy. After earning a bachelor's degree, she went on to pursue advanced degrees. She became a psychoanalyst. This was in the early 1960s, when few women earned advanced degrees. She spent her adult life helping others. When we began working together, she shared with me that despite all the study and work she had done, she felt powerless when it came to the story of her life. She believed that when it came to personal relationships, she did not have any choice but to be mistreated. Therefore she had chosen celibacy. She was also lonely. She shared that this was her reason for coming to me. After a few months of work, *she began to see that she was greater than her story* of being mistreated. I reflected to her that despite all the abuse she had endured as a child, she had tremendous courage. She had the courage to leave home even though her parents had expected her to remain with them. She had the courage to explore her sexual preference by being with women. She had the courage to choose a profession where she felt valued and respected. And I assured her that she had the courage to create a relationship that was different from her story. As she could take this in, she began to tap the powerful resources of truth within her. This helped her dissolve the negative belief that her story could define her. She began to see that while exploring her story helped her recover the truth about herself, it was not the truth of who she is. Now, in her early sixties, she decided to open to love again. She met a lovely woman, and the two of them have created a caring life together.

The trap our historical stories hold, as well the ones we make up daily, is that we have a limited repertoire. *We tend to repeat the same story over and over,* both in our experience and the telling of it. In other words, our stories (historical and current) are colored by our earlier experiences of our traumas, wounds, messages, beliefs, and defenses. We may change the backdrop, the characters, and the situation, but upon close investigation, *the kernel of the story is always the same.* And the repetition of the story and our emotions attached to it creates a biological event in our bodies. It programs our cells to expect the feelings attached to the story while reducing receptivity to something new and unknown.

Another client's repetitive story was that if something positive happened in his life, it was because God was favoring him. If something negative happened, it was because God was displeased. He felt that he always had to do something to regain or stay in God's favor. It did not matter if the telling of his story was about the weather, a situation at work, winning money, losing money, being sick or healthy. The essence of his story always boiled down to this: He was bad and he had to work very hard to convince God that he would be good. Whenever someone gave him a gift, he very quickly had to give something back so that God would see he was being good. He came to me exhausted. After we worked together for several months, he finally shared that he resented it when people gave him gifts. He did not feel joy in receiving them, he told me—he felt obligated.

As obstacles, *our stories are subjective.* They have a tenacious hold on how we experience and perceive life.

In believing that our stories are all there is and thus the ultimate reality, we end up cutting ourselves off from the fullness that life is offering. We are not experiencing what is objectively happening. *Through the lens of our stories, we are creating our own distorted spin.* This perpetuates and cements our emotional wound, negative messages, beliefs, and defense systems.

OBSTACLE #5: Believing Your Thoughts

> *"When the soul lies down in that grass,*
> *the world is too full to talk about.*
> *Ideas, language, even the phrase each other*
> *doesn't make any sense."* — Jalal-al-din Rumi

The final obstacle that stands between you and the truth of you are is that as humans, we tend to believe our thoughts without even questioning them. This may be a leap for some, but stay with me. Our mind does one thing and one thing only. It thinks. As humans, our capacity to think is necessary and when exercised consciously, a blessing. At the same time, our minds think incessantly and randomly, usually unconsciously, and most of our thoughts tend to be unkind, both toward others and ourselves. This is because all too often our minds have become fixed and closed. *A closed mind has no room for inquiry or a different perspective.* We end up believing our thoughts, even though they are typically the fearful shadows of our conditioned beliefs and perceptions.

Once you begin to observe your thoughts, you may become aware of this, as well as of the fact that thoughts are hitched to the past and future. Thoughts do not live in the absolute present moment of now. Direct experience, the illuminating consciousness that is you, is what lives in the present.

Thoughts are essential for maneuvering through life and recalling our stories to help us understand and heal. They are essential for making plans, envisioning goals, inquiry, discerning, problem solving, evolving, and inventing, but they do not assist us in being present in the moment. *You will learn over time that it is the felt sense within your body that brings you into the moment.* When you are in the present, the mind is free to be the witness, the lucid tool to perceive the illuminated consciousness of who you are and all that is.

"Through our eyes, the universe is perceiving itself. Through our ears, the universe is listening to its

harmonies. We are the witnesses through which the universe becomes conscious of its glory, of its magnificence." —Alan W. Watts

Now that you have a sense of the obstacles that stand between you and the truth of who you are, it is time to look at why we cling to them and how you can begin to heal and dissolve them. Chapter 3 takes a close look at that.

CHAPTER #2

The Key Points to Understanding Obstacles

1. The First Obstacle—The Trauma and the Wound: They are not obstacles in and of themselves. It is how we relate to them that creates the obstacle.

2. The Second Obstacle—Negative Messages: They fall into three categories: Parental, Societal, and Self-Generated. Negative Beliefs are the results of the negative messages.

3. The Third Obstacle—Defense Systems: Flight, Fight, or Freeze. Original purpose is to protect self to survive. Over time, these defense systems develop into habitual, unhealthy patterns, being used when there is no real threat. Judging separates. Judging is the glue of our beliefs and the cement of our defense systems.

4. The Fourth Obstacle—Believing Your Story is All There Is: There are two kinds of stories. The first is your perceptional recall and emotional experiences of your history. The second are the ones you make up each day. We let our stories define us. We tend to repeat them. Our subjective lens leads us to believe they are the only reality.

5. The Fifth Obstacle—Believing Your Thoughts: Thoughts are often repetitive and unkind. The mind becomes fixed and closed. Thoughts are connected to the past and future. The now is experienced as the felt sense.

6. Obstacles are the parts of the self that maintain (consciously or unconsciously) a sense of separation. They impede and stop the flow of spontaneity, of being open to the self and life in the present moment.

7. Obstacles are held in place by fear.

   - They are a part of the human condition at this stage of our evolution.
   - The first obstacle, the trauma and wound, create the foundation for obstacles 2 through 5.
   - In the Sleepwalking Phase, obstacles define your sense of self and reality. They are in charge. They are limiting. They are reactive. They are repetitive.
   - Over time, you will learn that while obstacles hold keys to self-understanding and transformation, they do not and cannot encompass reality and the truth of who you are.
   - Your relationship to your obstacles will change, grow, and heal as you progress through the Seven Phases of Human Consciousness in your life.
   - By the time, you reach the Committed Phase, you will understand that obstacles are part of the

experience of living in duality. They have become your teachers. As such, you will be able to relate to the obstacles more openly, with compassion and inquiry.

THE LIVING PRACTICE #2
Getting to Know Your Obstacles

Creating, Experiencing, Pause, Inquiry, and Transformation

After considering the Five Obstacles, spend some time with the following inquiry. As you inquire, pay attention to all the sensations within your physical body. It is within your body that all experience and transformation occurs.

1. Make a list of the obstacles as they are currently affecting your life. Put them in order from one to five, one being the most prominent in your current state of awareness, five being the least important in your awareness now. (You may notice as you journey on your path that the obstacles will probably shift in priority as you work through them.)

2. Write about the most prominent obstacle in your life. When did it begin? Why did it begin? Write about this in detail to yourself.

3. How does this obstacle define you and limit you and your view of life?

4. Were you aware of any emotions coming up for you as you read or wrote about the obstacles? If yes, what were they? Were you aware of where you felt the emotion in your body? Be as specific as possible, as this level of inquiry leads to insight and transformation.

5. Did one emotion take over? Or was there an ebb and flow of different emotions? Write about the emotions you were feeling in relationship to each of the obstacles and to the most prominent one in your life as you explored it.

6. If you did not experience an emotion(s), what were you aware of happening in your body during your inquiry? (For example, were you restless? relaxed?)

Inward Journey to Befriend the Obstacles

Find a comfortable place to sit or lie down. Close your eyes and focus on your breathing, noticing the state of your breathing... You might discover that your breath is shallow or fast or anxious or deep or quiet. After discovering the quality of your breathing, take three long, slow, deep breaths with the intention of opening and relaxing your body and your mind... If you are already relaxed, this will support you dropping even deeper into an opened state of awareness.

Now, imagine you are sitting at a table with six chairs. You begin to look around the table and you see that each of the five obstacles occupies a chair. You see your early childhood Trauma and Wound sitting in the first chair. The second chair holds your Negative Messages and Negative Beliefs. In the third chair are your Defenses and Judging. The fourth chair holds Believing Your Story is All There Is and Believing Your Thoughts is in the fifth chair. You are seated in the sixth chair. The obstacles are looking at you. They might look uncomfortable, angry, sad, anxious, or confused. Whatever they might look like on the surface, *underneath they are looking to you for help, for guidance.* In the center of the table is a beautiful white teapot filled with hot tea. Around the teapot are six cups with saucers and a tray of delicious, warm cookies. You reach out and, lifting the teapot, pour tea for each of the obstacles and yourself. You place the filled cups and a cookie in front of each chair and then you sit back down. Your tea and cookie are in front of you. You sip your tea slowly, taking in the soothing warmth. You take a bite of the cookie and enjoy its delicious, sweet taste. You feel your body relax as you sip your tea, and you feel your whole nervous system calm down. You look around the table. The obstacles are taking your lead, and they begin to sip their tea. As you continue to drink your tea, you feel the tension and confusion around the table in the obstacles begin to dissolve. You feel yourself sigh in relief, and you notice that the obstacles are also sighing in relief. You look at them and gently smile, aware now that, just like you, they are looking for healing. You open your arms and extending your hands toward them, say, 'Welcome friends.'

Gently bringing this journey to a close, focus again on your breath. Slowly open your eyes, and when you are ready, sit up. Spend some time writing about your experience of your journey. In particular, you may want to write about how it felt to connect with your obstacles in a different and perhaps new way.

Gently take in your surroundings before you stand up and go about the rest of your day.

An Affirmation to Help Heal the Obstacles
"I trust that each obstacle in my life comes as a sacred teacher, helping me to return to the truth of who I am."

3

OBSTACLES
AND
WHY WE CLING
TO THEM

"Here is the world.

Beautiful and terrible things will happen.

Don't be afraid."

—FREDERICK BUECHNER,
Beyond Words: Daily Readings in the ABC's of Faith

FEAR LIVES AT THE ROOT OF ALL OBSTACLES

One of my clients spent his first year working with me, insisting that what I was offering as a way to heal, might apply to others but not to him. His life had been spent being ridiculed and ostracized for being physically disabled. He had suffered a spinal cord injury as a young child and was confined to a wheelchair. He was angry and hurt. He was afraid. He felt defective. How could I offer him a way out of his suffering if there was something inherently wrong with him? In our work together, we explored the pain that life had dealt him. We looked at the fact that while none of us have control over some of the events in our life and how others treat us, we have control over how we use that to limit or heal us. Over time, he began to see that while the obstacles kept him safe, they also kept him alone and unhappy. The purpose of this chapter is to look at *obstacles as blocks to our freedom and happiness*. And in doing so, how we can learn to use them as steppingstones to return to the freedom that the truth offers.

If the truth is liberating, then why do we resist it? One person might resist the truth from fear that they might change so much they may leave their job, spouse, or current friends, or that their spouse and friends might leave them. Someone else might resist because they are afraid to re-visit and feel a painful event from their past. While there may be many different reasons why we resist, essentially, we block the truth out of fear. Fear is at the root of all obstacles.

EXPLORING NEGATIVE MESSAGES AND BELIEFS AS AN EXAMPLE OF WHY WE CLING TO OBSTACLES

We will use the second obstacle, Negative Messages and Beliefs, to look at why we tend to cling to obstacles.

To begin with, many of us have gotten the message that there is something wrong with us, and in turn we have come to believe that. As stated earlier, the bottom-line belief that much of humanity clings to is "I'm bad." As a result, throughout our lives we may have told ourselves:

"Because children tease me, I'm bad.
Because my mother hits me, I'm bad.
Because I have a physical disability or illness I'm bad.
Because my boyfriend left me, I'm bad.

Because I didn't get the job I want, I'm bad.

Because my religion says so, I'm bad."

...and the list goes on and on.

We hold on to these beliefs because the creation of them was based on a conclusion from an even deeper, and false, belief. That belief is, "When bad things happen, or when good things don't happen, I am at fault because there is something wrong with me." We tell ourselves:

"If I were good,

Children would play with me,

My mother would hug me,

I would not have a physical disability,

My boyfriend would stay,

I would get the job I want,

My religion would say that I am good

just the way I am."

OBSTACLES BEGIN FORMING IN CHILDHOOD

Keeping with our example, our false beliefs arise out of both the collective misunderstandings held within humanity and our own early childhood experiences.

During your early experiences, a part of the psyche called the child consciousness is formed. It is a part of *your psyche that froze and separated within you at the time of your early trauma and wound*. In other words, your child consciousness is the age you were when the trauma and wound occurred in your life. For example, if the trauma you experienced happened when you were six months old, the age of the emotional wound and therefore child consciousness within you is that of a six-month-old. The emotional wound and subsequent negative belief experienced at such a young age is a felt sense, it cannot be explained in rational terms.

It is important that we as adults understand this. When we deny the right of the child consciousness to exist within us, it is like telling a six-month-old baby that it doesn't have the right to be scared or angry or sad when it is experiencing being abandoned, unloved, and so on. The felt sense at such early ages is often experienced as a matter of life or death.

Also as an adult, a current traumatic or unpleasant experience may really be happening, or the adult may be experiencing a fear-filled projection. Whatever is happening with the adult, the child consciousness within them is experiencing it as if it is real and as if they are again caught in a matter of life or death.

Since the belief arose very early in your experience as a felt sense, your child consciousness can get triggered when life doesn't happen the way you want or the way you believe it needs to happen for you to feel safe or good about yourself. Thus, life experiences are often used to fuel our negative beliefs. Going back to our previous example, if as an adult, you have an experience of not getting the job you want, you may internally experience it from the child consciousness, and thus believe, "I didn't get the job because I'm bad. There is something wrong with me."

I am convinced that if we could take a photograph of a group of adults and show what is emotionally going on, we would see a lot of children in grown-up bodies. With that as a parameter, it is easy to find reasons to qualify the negative beliefs about ourselves. When we find, or create reasons, the obstacle is further cemented. You can probably find several reasons every day to confirm your negative beliefs. The constant barrage of life experiences can cement our beliefs. Being stuck in those beliefs blocks us from experiencing the truth of who we are. As a friend shared, beliefs are like leashes. We hold on to a belief and are only open to life, as far the leash will allow.

WE CLING TO OBSTACLES BECAUSE THEY ARE FAMILIAR

Second to that, our negative beliefs are familiar. They slid into place very early in our lives, and not only do they "seem" right, they just "feel" right. As human beings, we typically gravitate to the familiar. It feels safe because it is known. If you were to release a negative belief that you have held as part of your identity, that part, of what you have believed about yourself would dissolve. This change could be uncomfortable, because it's new. It's unknown. The unknown terrifies many people. Most people are more comfortable with a certain degree of discomfort or suffering rather than exposing themselves to the new.

(Pause for a moment to consider: Who would you be and how might you emotionally feel if you stopped believing that there is something wrong with you? What do you experience in your body as you contemplate this possibility?)

Thirdly, some of us cling to our negative beliefs because we experience a perverse sense of satisfaction or negative pleasure when we feel the familiarity of our belief being confirmed. The pleasure current is an integral part of the overall life force current. If we don't have access to its positive expression, we will find ways to experience it negatively. Using our, "I didn't get the job I wanted" example, we might say, "Here I am again, I never get what I want, there really is something wrong with me." While saying that, we might feel a current of familiarity that is pleasurable. I say pleasurable in the sense that such thoughts can be comforting, because, if negative beliefs are true, then there is really nothing we can do to change things. And if that is true, we might as well stick with the negative but familiar and comfortable belief.

WE CLING TO OBSTACLES BECAUSE HEALING THEM REQUIRES CHANGE

Additionally, we stick with our negative beliefs because if we were to begin healing them, we would have to change. Part of change requires that we feel the emotional pain of the negative belief and when and how these beliefs were created in the first place. We would also have to feel our grief for the betrayal we felt from those who helped foster the beliefs and the grief of our continued self-betrayal in believing them.

Change also requires that we become responsible for ourselves and our choices. Change would mean leaving the familiar, victim state of helplessness that is held by negative beliefs. Becoming responsible offers us the opportunity to harness our courage and motivation to change.

WE CLING TO OBSTACLES BECAUSE THEY ARE HARD-WIRED

Finally, we hold on to our negative beliefs because, over time, they become hard-wired. Even at the cellular level, such as in our nervous and endocrine systems, we hold on to these beliefs.

Rewiring our internal network takes time and patience. Imagine rewiring the entire electrical system in your home. It would be a massive undertaking. Similarly, "rewiring" ourselves and healing our negative beliefs is no small task. Since many people are impatient and want instant results or immediate gratification, they default to the hard-wired beliefs rather than devote themselves to the challenge of change and healing.

"I was exhilarated by the new realization that I could change the character of my life by changing my beliefs.

I was instantly energized because I realized that there was a science-based path that would take me from my job as a perennial 'victim' to my new position as 'co-creator' of my destiny."
—Bruce H. Lipton, The Biology of Belief

While we have used negative beliefs as our example when examining why we cling to obstacles, remember, all that has been written applies to each of the obstacles. The tradeoff for staying attached to the obstacles is an adjusted, resigned suffering instead of the courage, introspection, and patience necessary to shift our wiring.

(Pause for a moment to consider: How many times have you listened to someone complain about a problem over and over and end their complaining by saying, "Oh well, I can't do anything about it." What did you experience inside of yourself as you listened to them? Did you want to give advice? Did you consider that perhaps you too, have done the same thing?)

No matter what is going on in your life, you have power over one thing: Your approach and your attitude toward what is happening. By staying committed to the work, these obstacles will dissolve, and you will come to recognize their divine purpose. Remember, obstacles are also part of the path.

HEALING AND DISSOLVING THE OBSTACLES

> *"Life begins at the end of your comfort zone."*
> —Neale Donald Walsch

If we are so invested in holding on to the obstacles that block us from the light inside us, how do we heal them? The obstacles within us are healed as we move through the Seven Phases. These include accepting the fact that we have obstacles; exploring the origin of them in our lives; the impact of these obstacles; our participation in creating them; feeling our feelings about them; and, eventually, letting go of the power they have on us.

Sang, a client of mine, came from China as a young child with her family. She was the second child and a girl. She was born at a time when mothers were shunned and fines had to be paid for having more than one child, especially when that child was female. As a little girl, Sang would often be made to sit quietly by herself for hours in a room so that she would not interfere with her mother's chores. Her uncle, the family patriarch, called her nasty names. Her parents never stepped in to protect her from his cruelty. Her mother never told Sang she loved her. Instead, she would hit her and yell at her, even after Sang became an adult. Out of these experiences, Sang formed the belief that she was unworthy of being loved. She married a man who did not love her but felt they should be together out of cultural duty. Several years into the marriage, she fell and dislocated her shoulder. Her husband refused to take care of her. That event, followed by a refusal to help her pursue an advanced degree, was a catalyst for Sang. She finally got the courage to leave her loveless marriage. Later, she became involved with a man who manipulated, ridiculed, and controlled her. She formed her whole life around him, meeting with him when and where it suited him. Sang started coming to me for sessions at that time. She felt she loved this man, but could not understand why he was so controlling. She was in a lot of pain. After talking about her sadness, Sang began looking at why she kept ending up in relationships where there was cruelty and shame.

We began by looking at the negative belief she carried deep within her—the belief that she was unlovable. Sang had grown up believing that the cruelty inflicted upon her was due to a deficiency in her. For many years, she had not even questioned whether this might not be true. When the pain was too great, she would deny that the origin of the problem might lie in those around her and not in her. Then, when the dam inside of her broke, she began to feel the pain. That is when she reached out for help.

As we talked about her shifting awareness over time, I introduced Sang to the Seven Phases of Human Consciousness. As she began to understand the different phases and her movement in them, she also began to see how they supported the dissolving of the obstacles within her. She also came to understand that the phases were an inherent, progressive transformation; instrumental in helping her find her way back to herself—a woman of courage and light.

In the next chapter, we will continue with Sang to introduce you to the Seven Phases of Human Consciousness. You will learn how you can use the phases to track your own transformation and how you can heal the obstacles in your path by moving through the phases.

CHAPTER #3

The Key Points to Obstacles and Why We Cling To Them

1. Fear is at the root of obstacles.

2. Obstacles block our happiness and life flow.

3. Obstacles begin in childhood.

4. When we are adults, obstacles are maintained and reinforced by child consciousness.

5. Child consciousness is the part of your psyche that separated within you at the time of your early trauma and wound.

6. From early childhood, the formation of obstacles is a cascading, circular, and patterning event. The cycles go like this:

    From trauma to the resulting emotional wound they begin to form,

    To the negative messages that are also wounding,

    To the negative beliefs that consequently arise,

    To the habitual defenses used to protect against feeling the pain of the wound and to protect your sense of self,

    To the constant judging that promotes separation

and is a defense against feeling the pain,

To believing that your story is the absolute truth,

To believing your thoughts, which are conditioned to support your stories about your trauma, wound, messages, beliefs, defenses, and judging.

This is how obstacles become repetitive, familiar, reinforced, hard-wired, and circular.

7. We cling to obstacles because they are familiar. Familiarity creates an identity and an illusion of safety.
8. We cling to obstacles because to heal them requires change.
9. To let go of clinging to obstacles would mean opening to the unknown. This is terrifying for many people.
10. We heal obstacles by:
    a. Accepting that they are part of our human experience.
    b. Exploring the origins of them in our life.
    c. Inquiring into our participation in creating and maintaining them.
    d. Changing our relationship to them.
    e. Understanding them with a clear mind and a compassionate heart.
    f. Feeling the painful feelings connected to them.
    g. Progressing through the Seven Phases.

THE LIVING PRACTICE #3
Exploring Obstacles

Creating, Experiencing, Pause, Inquiry, and Transformation

Why you cling to obstacles and the role of fear in your life
Find a quiet place for contemplation while considering the following questions:

1. Where do you feel stuck or blocked in your life?

2. Can you relate where you feel stuck, to a specific obstacle? Which obstacle is it? Now, let's do some inquiry with the obstacle you have chosen.

3. Can you feel your investment or attachment to this obstacle?

4. Why are you attached to it? Sit with open curiosity and notice any sensations in your body; be aware of emotions that might arise, thoughts, or images you might see.

5. How is your attachment to this obstacle serving or protecting you?

6. Imagine for a moment letting go of this obstacle. Do you experience any fear as you consider this possibility? If yes, can you sense where you experience this fear in your body? What is this fear about? (Stay in open inquiry.)

7. How old is this fear?

8. If this fear could speak to you, what would it say? Letting our emotions speak to us as if they were another person can be a powerful way to hear clearly what is going on inside of us and, often surprisingly, what our unmet needs are. So, let the fear underneath the obstacle have its own voice—let your pencil or computer flow as fear conveys itself.

Inward Journey to Experience Yourself Free of the Obstacles

Find a comfortable place to sit or, preferably, lie down. Close your eyes and focus on your breathing, noticing the state of your breathing.... You might discover that your breath is shallow or fast or anxious or deep or quiet. After discovering the quality of your breathing, take three long, slow, deep breaths with the intention to open and relax your body and your mind.... If you are already relaxed, this will support you dropping even deeper into an opened state of awareness.

Now, imagine you are in a room filled with the light. You look for the source of the light and you see that it is coming from a luminescent figure standing in front of you. You can't see who it is; you can only see this beautiful light radiating from them toward you. Continue to look at the light.... Allow it to permeate and nourish you. Allow the light to enter the places of tension in your body, dissolving any worries you might be having, soothing any upsetting feelings you might be experiencing....

As you continue to let the light in, you realize that the figure is moving toward you. The closer s/he gets to you, the clearer their image....

When their image is completely clear, you see that the light-filled figure is *You*. With arms outstretched, your light-filled self is welcoming you.... You walk toward yourself and you feel the homecoming when you embrace...you feel joy and peace as the two of you; your light-filled, illuminated self and you the journeyer, become one.

Your body is opened and relaxed... Your mind is clear, your emotions flow in a peaceful, uninterrupted way. Your breathing is steady and calm. Feel the breath in your body, filled with light, nourishing every cell of your being with the flow of life... Just relax in this place for a few more minutes, feeling this truth: *You are the light.* You are free of all the obstacles that have stood in the way between you and this direct experience of the truth of who you are....

Gently bringing this journey to a close, focus again on your breath. Slowly open your eyes and when you are ready, sit up. Spend some time writing about your experience of the journey. In particular, you may want to write about what it was like to feel yourself free of obstacles.

Gently take in your surroundings before you stand up and go about the rest of your day.

An Affirmation to Support
Your Healing of the Obstacles

"As I work through the obstacles, I am open to the whole me. I accept and love all of who I am."

PART TWO
The Journey

4

INTRODUCING THE SEVEN PHASES OF HUMAN CONSCIOUSNESS

*"Wisdom says we are nothing.
Love says we are everything.
Between these two our life flows."*

—JACK KORNFIELD

During our work together, Sang worked through the Seven Phases of Human Consciousness. These *phases are aspects of consciousness or levels of awareness in human life*. Some people spend their entire life within one phase. Others are born at a progressed phase. Most of us need to pass through each of the Seven Phases on our healing journey home to the truth of who we are. Within each phase there are *gradual shifts in movement, insight, and growth*.

It is important to note that *we don't move through these phases in a linear fashion*. The path does not go directly from phase one to seven. We may go from one to four and back to three and then leap to six and so on. In other words, as you begin to address an issue in your life, one that you had previously denied or pretended did not exist, you may return to denying it at some later point. For instance, I have moved in and out of the Denial Phase in relationship to my feelings about my body. Sometimes I have done the deep work of meeting and resolving the pain in me about what I experienced as the early disapproval of my body. At other times, I have gone back into denial about the effect that negative message has had on me.

Alternatively, you may be in one phase in certain aspects of your life and in another phase with other aspects or issues. As an example, you may be in the Denial Phase regarding your sexuality and in the Committed Phase with your profession. Also, as you work through your denial about one issue, you may still live in denial with another issue—one that you have not thought about. Think of the *movement of your growth as a spiral.* You go around and around, touching the same wounds, beliefs etc... Yet as you consciously move through the phases, you are not going in a circle and recycling. You are spiraling—going deeper—increasing your understanding and compassion as you gently heal.

FORGETTING AND REMEMBERING

The sequence of Phases is divided into two distinct aspects of living and healing. These sequences are **"The Forgetting"** and **"The Remembering."**

Forgetting is when we live without awareness that a deep internal life awaits us, unaware that we are magnificent and that we have a creative say in our lives, our choices, our destiny. *Forgetting is living life from a reactive, repetitive place.* In Forgetting, *we live in fear* of ourselves, others, and life. In forgetting, we do not realize that we are an integral part of the whole and that all life; all aspects of creation are miraculous and filled with wonder. We do not realize our interdependency with all life. We are unaware that our thoughts, feelings, and actions have consequence and that how we live affects all of life. We experience ourselves as separate. In my twenties, during an extended illness I lived in fear and hopelessness. I could not fathom that there was a bright light in me, just waiting to be recognized and freed. I had forgotten. In the forgetting phase, we have forgotten the truth of who we are and all that is, until one day we decide enough is enough. We have grown tired of fear, suffering, and close-mindedness. We long for depth, freedom, and internal happiness.

That is when we are ready to take on the work of remembering. *Glorious remembering.* Our souls, starved and parched from lack of deep nourishment and fulfillment, hunger for the light, the truth within us. *To remember, we must turn to face ourselves and search deep within.* We need to liberate ourselves from the shackles that the obstacles have defined as us and return to the light within—the light that has always been there. When I became tired of being sick and tired, I was ready to make the effort to begin the work of remembering. I did this by making new choices for myself, seeking guidance, getting professional support, and believing that with perseverance, I would be able to create real happiness inside of myself. You can create happiness, too!

It is important to note that *remembering* means the truth is *inside of you*. You have forgotten. That's all. An essential part of you has always held this knowledge. You are now in the process of accessing that part of you that has held the truth of who you are. It has been waiting for you to return, to remember, and reclaim your magnificent Self. It really is that simple. Thus, the work of the last five phases is necessary for dissolving each obstacle.

HERE ARE THE PHASES:
Forgetting:

1. **Sleepwalking**—You are unconscious, living life on the surface, from the exterior, unaware that a deep inner life exists within you. You are completely attached to the obstacles as if they are the ultimate reality. You are focused on reacting to situations and people around you.

2. **Denial**—You may be aware of feeling discomfort and suffering about the life issues in you and around you. But you subconsciously deceive or lie to yourself by avoiding them, pretending they don't exist. You are still focused on the "drama" around you, as if that is the only cause of your suffering.

Remembering:

3. **SOS (Help! Crisis!)**—You feel distress signals inside yourself. You may be in crisis. You are at the tipping point. You are tired of suffering, and you want to be out of pain, no matter if it requires you to change. And it does!

4. **Knowledge and Resources**—You begin gathering resources and acquiring knowledge by reading, seeking professional help, educating yourself, and finding support groups and mentors to help you with your pain and suffering. You also begin to access your inner resources. You begin to glimpse the possibility of healing.

5. **Opening**—You have the courage to open and feel the pain (mental, emotional, physical, spiritual) and suffering that have blocked you. You are beginning to understand the origin of the obstacles inside you and the pain connected with them. Through releasing the emotions of anger and grief, you begin to experience the wellspring of joy, love, and peace within you.

6. **Committed**—Each day becomes a life unto itself. This means *each day* is an opportunity for you to engage in the Living Practice of creating, experiencing, pause, inquiry, and transformation. You have developed a reflective inner life. You accept responsibility for your choices, your life. You are more prone to positive action. You are doing the daily work of healing the obstacles within you. You are learning how to move from reaction to response. You are experiencing greater moments of awakening to the truth of who you are. You are spiritually maturing. You no longer endure life. Life has become an adventure, a mystical classroom through which you transform into the

creative light being you are. You love life enough to understand that all life experiences, both positive and negative, serve an awakening purpose. You know that all the deep inner work you do is not only in service to yourself but to all of creation.

7. **Illumination**—You are Awakened, Pure Consciousness, Self-Realized, the great witness of creation in divine play. You are enlivened, embodied, playful, joyful, peacefully awakened in the moment. Each breath, each being, each experience is new and miraculous. There is a complete absence of having to know what the next moment will be. The limiting negative ego identity has dissolved along with the obstacles, while the positive aspects of the human ego are used as tools to peacefully navigate through time and space. You directly experience the infinite love and light within you and all of creation. You live and yet are not attached to the form of living. You are fully established in the supreme truth and you have become One, or as Kahlil Gibran wrote in *The Prophet,* "Self is a sea boundless and measureless."

SANG'S JOURNEY THROUGH THE SEVEN PHASES

We will use the example of the second obstacle, negative beliefs, to follow Sang's movement through the Seven Phases and how this movement helped her dissolve her negative belief of being unlovable. We will see how the phases brought her closer to seeing her true self and to loving herself.

THE FIRST PHASE:
Sleepwalking

This phase is a dwelling place for many. Many adults unknowingly live their lives asleep. *To sleepwalk means to live life without inquiry.* It means to unconsciously bury painful experiences, traumas, and wounds, the negative messages and beliefs. It means to accept external experiences and situations of your life as the absolute reality. Essentially, sleepwalking is a very effective defense. It is important to note that sleepwalking is okay. It is simply the first phase of human consciousness.

This first phase does not refer to the chronology of age. Many infants and small children are born or live in an advanced phase. When traumas and difficult life experiences cannot be assimilated, children may begin to mute their light, to shut down and, essentially, go to sleep. This reversal may increase through childhood and puberty, until as adults they have firmly ensconced themselves into the Sleepwalking Phase.

Part of our journey as spiritual beings incarnating into the human experience is that our souls create a type of amnesia. This is done to create the groundwork for the misunderstandings our souls have specifically come to heal. Having been given free will, each person is then free to choose how to spend his or her life. Some may focus their life with the intention to heal, evolve, and transform, and some may spend it sleepwalking. That said, for those who choose to spend their life in forgetting, each person will reach the point in their soul's evolution, whether in this lifetime or another, where they want to go deeper, they *want to remember.*

Sang had a very painful childhood. She buried her grief and anger about being mistreated and unloved. Without questioning, she obeyed the familial and cultural demands required of her as a woman. She believed that this was the reality of life—no more, no less. She believed that she was unlovable. Many of our negative beliefs are formed in the

Sleepwalking Phase. As one friend observed, beliefs are like leashes. We hold on to them, and we go only as far as the leash allows. In sleepwalking, people live on very short leashes.

> "The mass of men lead lives of quiet desperation"
> —Henry David Thoreau,
> *Civil Disobedience and Other Essays*

At the urging of her soul, gradually, after many painful years, Sang wanted something more. She had no idea what that was, she just knew that there had to be more than just life on the surface.

THE SECOND PHASE:
Denial

Denial is often misunderstood. A popular view of denial is that a person does not know that the pain and suffering about an issue or issues exists. That view describes sleepwalking. Denial occurs when the person knows or senses there is discomfort or pain about an issue, but instead chooses to pretend, contradict, or reject that anything is wrong, at least *with them*. In some circles, *denial is described as an elephant standing in the middle of the room while everyone in the room pretends it isn't there.*

After Sang dislocated her shoulder and experienced the hurt of her husband's refusal to care for her, she went to stay at her parent's house. Her mother allowed her to stay, but only with very strict rules. Those rules included that Sang had to wash her own clothes. Sang had to do this with the use of only one arm. After two days, her mother sent Sang home. Sang shared with me how painful it was that her mother had treated her so unkindly. She also shared that she chose to deny this because the pain was too much for her to feel at the time. Back home, she took care of her family with one arm in a brace, because her husband demanded that their lives continue as normal. She would not talk with anyone about the neglect she experienced during that time. She went to Sunday family dinners at her parents' house and acted like nothing had happened. Her family acted like that too. In other words, Sang was living in denial.

The hopeful thing about denial is that the truth lives right underneath it. The truth always shines, even though it may be blocked from view. The light of truth will occasionally penetrate denial. So, every now and then, the soul of the person in denial will help the person to feel the sharp touch of truth. When that happens, the pain that has been buried surfaces to be felt, even if fleetingly.

Eventually, there is more pain than denial, and the person is ready to change. For Sang, that moment came when she spoke with her husband about going back to school to earn her master's degree. When he told her that he did not believe it was right for her to pursue a higher education and that he would not pay for her education, denial finally slipped away. Sang began to feel the deep sadness inside of her. In feeling it, she began to realize that this pain had been in her for a very long time.

THE THIRD PHASE: SOS (Crisis! Help!)

This is the phase when people usually seek help. Their pain and suffering have become too much. They are often tormented, in acute distress, and desperately want to be out of it. They are in spiritual crisis, or the *Dark Night of the Soul*, as written about in a poem by Saint John of the Cross in the sixteenth century. Life as they have lived it is meaningless. It doesn't make sense anymore. They are experiencing an 'identity crisis." This level of distress *creates a willingness to do something new.* This phase initiates a return to remembering the truth. It requires tremendous courage, because change means taking risks. It means letting go of the life we know and moving into unknown territory. It means the willingness to stop clinging so tightly to the obstacles that have stood in the way of truth.

In my twenties, I spent almost four years in and out of hospitals, in and out of surgery for a disease that was the result of wearing a birth-control device. I was so broken back then, hurting deeply but denying it. I was also a smoker. In those days, you could smoke in hospitals. On the day after my last surgery, a radical hysterectomy at the age of twenty-seven, I lay in bed, clutching my belly as I attempted to smoke. I started coughing. My abdomen hurt as I coughed. I looked at the cigarette in one hand while my other hand held my belly, trying to manage the pain. That was my tipping point. I "got" the craziness of what we as humans often do to avoid our deep emotional pain. We will endure all sorts of other pain, such as physical pain or the pain of unfulfillment, hopelessness, and despair. All too often, we accept these types of pain as the condition of living rather than take the risk to open and change. In that moment of realization, I moved out of denial and into the SOS Phase. I threw the cigarette away and never smoked again. I wanted to be out of pain, no matter what.

For Sang, her SOS moment followed her husband's refusal to support her dream to become a psychologist. She had two young children. She lived in a culture that did not support a woman's right to choose her own destiny, let alone defy her husband. With infinite courage, Sang filed for divorce and took out a loan to go to graduate school. She had finally reached the point where the pain of being unloved and mistreated every day of her life was just wrong. She was ready to change.

THE FOURTH PHASE:
Knowledge and Resources

When you plan a trip to another country, an unknown place, there is much preparation needed. You may buy maps, translation dictionaries, and books about where to go and what to see. *You are eager to gather resources and acquire knowledge.* You pour through them seeking direction, guidance, and understanding. The path back to the truth of who you are is the same. In this phase, when you are finally ready to change, you may gobble up volumes of books that relate to what you want to change and heal in yourself, your life. You may seek out groups with similar goals. You may search for a therapist, mentor, or coach who can meet you where you are and help guide the way for you at this stage of your journey.

After returning home from the hospital, I told my mother that if I did not get professional help, I would jump out the window. I did not mean it literally. I just knew that I was desperate. I needed to make a strong statement in order to be taken seriously about my need for outside resources. One of my sisters helped me find my first therapist. To this day, I credit that therapist with saving my life.

For Sang, going to graduate school to become a psychologist was her doorway into the Knowledge and Resource Phase. It ignited her quest for human understanding and showed her the beginning steps of how to heal. From there she started therapy to help heal the pain of her childhood. She had also tapped into one of her own inner resources, courage. Additionally, she found a program that helped support her personal transformation.

THE FIFTH PHASE:
Opening

All the uncomfortable feelings from the early emotional trauma and wound, the subsequent negative messages received, and limited beliefs formed as a result *need to be felt and released*. All the defenses, denial, and stories that have protected you from feeling need to be loosened. In this phase, you are ready to feel. I tell my students, feeling equals healing.

When secure and safe, children naturally respond to painful situations by feeling and expressing those feelings as they are happening. When a child feels unsafe or the experience is too great to process, those feelings go underground. As adults, we are conditioned to wear a mask and pretend that everything is okay. *We have learned to block the natural flow of feelings.* On top of that, many of us have been taught that some feelings (joy, happiness, love) are okay and that others (grief, anger, fear, frustration) are not. Therefore, *part of opening is to feel the buried feelings.*

In this phase, Sang began to feel. During that time, she also began seeing me for support. At first Sang hesitated to go deeply into her feelings. She was afraid of what might happen if she started to feel. She would ask me, "Aren't these feelings bad? Will I be out of control, will I hurt myself or someone else?" These are often the fears we use to keep our uncomfortable feelings silent. I assured Sang that I was there to support her and that safely releasing these feelings would help her to heal. When she was ready, we started to work with her feelings of rage, which at the time were predominantly focused on her mother. In one session, she hit pillows and screamed and cried about all the cruelty she had experienced as a child. At the end of that session, Sang felt freer and began to feel compassion for herself. Many months later in her healing, Sang also began to feel compassion for her mother. Part of what begins to happen in this phase is forgiveness: forgiving yourself for the self-inflicted hatred and betrayal and forgiveness toward others for their actions that fostered the wounding. We begin to realize that those who hurt us are also wounded, and that their actions arose out of their own misunderstandings and obstacles. Thus, *genuine forgiveness* occurs after we have allowed ourselves to feel. We then have the emotional space within us for other feelings and other perspectives. In other words, when we have a greater capacity to be ourselves, we have a greater capacity to understand and accept others as they are.

While the initial way Sang released her anger and grief was from hitting pillows, *there are many safe ways to open, feel, and release.* Hitting pillows while powerful may not be the right way for some people.

THE SIXTH PHASE:
Committed

The American author Somerset Maugham titled his book *The Razor's Edge,* after a Katha Upanishads verse, "Rise, wake up, seek the wise and realize. The path is difficult to cross like the sharpened edge of the razor, so say the wise." This verse invites inquiry and several interpretations. One interpretation being that it is easy to fall off the razor thin path, back into a state of *forgetting.* That said, one can also get back on to the path by simply *remembering.* In the commitment phase, this awareness is important. *Commitment is not about perfection.* Rather, it is the intention and willingness to engage daily life as a living practice of expanding self-awareness, creating, inquiry, forgiveness, transformation and love. Living your life with commitment will open you to experiencing miracles that are present in even the smallest of details. It will open you to viewing your life experiences and the obstacles inside you as unending opportunities for healing and growth. *In this phase, life as you knew it really begins to change. You will realize that you and all life are a dynamic process*, a beautiful verb, shifting, changing, fluid. This is when your heart truly begins to fully open, and the judgments that kept you separate in the past start to dissolve. You begin to experience gratitude and acceptance for all that is. It is through commitment to doing the work of remembering that you receive the grace-filled awareness that you are a being of light, expressed as love and experienced as joy and peace.

Sang's life has substantially transformed during her time in the Committed Phase. While she has had notable external changes, such as a boyfriend who is respectful and kind, continued growth in her profession as a psychologist, and a loving family environment with her children and dogs, the biggest changes have been internal. Sang actively uses the Living Practice tools, and as a result is better able to respond to life rather than react. She has become compassionate toward herself. She has forgiven her parents, and while accepting them as they are, she has learned to hold healthy boundaries for herself and her children in relation to them.

THE SEVENTH PHASE:
Illumination

I initially hesitated writing about this phase. For some, this phase may appear unrealistic, unattainable. However, *Illumination is the ultimate destination for each soul.* It is the Awakened Self, fully at home within Spirit/Source. It is the *no-self* state of awareness. It is as empty and as full as the infinite sky—at the same time. The purpose of this book is not to drive you to this goal. To do so might create a field of disappointment.

Instead, I recommend that you simply commit *to doing the work* of remembering the truth of you are. Let the ultimate phase, Illumination, take care of itself. For surely, Illumination in its constant, unwavering state of awareness will come in its own perfect timing for you. When your soul is complete, integrated, and has healed all misunderstandings, and when you are completely present in the NOW, you will experience the Self and its oceanic state of Pure Consciousness. From this vantage point, the Self can see clearly and witness the light in everyone and everything. You become the peaceful observer of All That Is. It is the arrival point after much ardent journeying. For Buddha, his homecoming took place under the Bodhi Tree.

When and where your homecoming will occur, who knows? However, it is in that Enlightened, moment-to-moment state you shall live.

> *One instant is eternity;*
> *eternity is the now.*
> *When you see through this one instant,*
> *You see through the one who sees."*
>
> —Wu-Men, *The Enlightened Heart:*
> *An Anthology of Sacred Poetry,*
> *edited* by Stephen Mitchell

In the meantime, as you do the work, you will be graced with glimpses and direct experiences of this truth. These glimpses have been how Sang, up to this point, has experienced Illumination. Meanwhile, she continues to live her life committed to her path of Awakening.

One of my spiritual teachers, Swami Muktananda, had been known to say, "Source, God, Pure Consciousness, is always pouring the light of Grace into you. You are just at a stage in your development where you cannot hold it. It slips through your fingers like water." This is how the work of Remembering functions. It is unwavering in its constant flow of truth and Grace. Your job is to stay steadfast. Show up for yourself and life, keep the faith, and do the work of healing the obstacles as you move through the Seven Phases of Consciousness.

As we move through chapters five through eleven, we will explore each phase in greater detail. You will discover how your relationship to the obstacles shifts and heals as you progress through the phases, awakening you to the truth of who you are!

CHAPTER #4

The Key Points to the Seven Phases

1. The Seven Phases indicate degrees of self-awareness.
2. We don't move through the phases linearly.
3. Within each phase are gradual shifts in movement, insight, and growth.
4. We may be in one phase in certain parts of our life and in another phase in other parts.
5. We may retreat to a previous phase with certain issues, particularly those that have had the greatest impact or those that hold an important key to our soul's growth within this lifetime.
6. The Seven Phases are divided into two sequences: Forgetting and Remembering. The first two phases (Sleepwalking and Denial) are in the Forgetting sequence. The remaining five phases (SOS, Knowledge and Resources, Opening, Committed, and Illumination) are in the Remembering sequence.
7. The Forgetting sequence is bound by separation, fear, reactivity, and repetition or habit.
8. The Remembering sequence requires you to turn inward, to search and inquire deeply within the self, learning to respond, to be in the unknown.

9. A longing and willingness to grow and to make new choices is essential for you to progress through the Phases.
10. Remembering means that the Truth you seek lives inside of you!

THE LIVING PRACTICE #4
The Seven Phases

Creating, Experiencing, Pause, Inquiry, and Transformation

Becoming Familiar with the Seven Phases

Find a quiet place for contemplation while creating the following:

1. Get a large piece of paper. On it, draw a long horizontal line that will indicate the timeline of your life. Mark the beginning of the timeline with your birth and the end of the timeline with your current age. Spend some time considering the important events of your life. These might include births, deaths, illnesses, significant events, relationships, accomplishments, challenges—really, only you know the important events of your life. As you recall them, draw vertical lines through your timeline with the age at which the event occurred above the line and the nature of the event directly below the corresponding age.

2. After you have finished your timeline, I want you to spend some reflective time in quiet contemplation. Which event in your life is calling for your attention

in this moment? Spend some time journaling why you have chosen this event.

3. Which phase do you resonate with the most in relation to the event? Once you have identified the phase as it corresponds to your chosen event, spend some time journaling why you feel you are in this phase in relationship to the event. See if you can correlate the phase with the sequence of either Forgetting or Remembering

4. If you were to progress to another phase in relation to the event, what steps do you think/feel you need to take to do so?

Inward Journey of Traveling Through the Seven Phases
Find a comfortable place to lie down. Close your eyes and focus on your breathing, just noticing the state of your breathing... You might discover that your breath is shallow or fast or anxious or deep or quiet. After discovering the quality of your breathing, take a few long, slow, deep breaths with the intention to open and relax your body and your mind. If you are already relaxed, this will support you dropping even deeper into an opened state of awareness.

In this journey, you will observe your life in relationship to the Seven Phases, as if you were watching a movie, to familiarize yourself with your current relationship to the phases. Pay attention to what you physically and emotionally experience as you move through the phases.

Phase 1: Sleepwalking... Imagine watching your life as if everything is happening *to you*, not in you. You see yourself reacting to situations and events without even considering your participation as co-creator. Give yourself time to watch...Phase 2: Denial ...you see yourself feeling unsettled for a moment as you are realizing that you may be a participant in creating the events or situations...you immediately deny it... Phase 3: SOS.... you see yourself suffering and lost in all the painful situations and events about yourself and your life. You decide you've had enough and you want to change. See yourself making this decision... Phase 4: Knowledge and Resources... Observe yourself reaching out to people for help, reading books, finding groups that are focused on healing the pain you experience in your self and in your life. Also take time to look inside yourself for one of your natural inner resources like courage or patience... Phase 5: Opening.... watch yourself open to feeling the painful emotions you have kept buried inside for so long. You may see yourself crying or yelling in anger.... after a few minutes, you see yourself feeling softer and in peace after releasing loss, grief, anger... Phase 6: Committed...see yourself wholeheartedly involved in the daily practice of co-creating, experiencing, pausing, inquiring, watch yourself dedicated to your own transformation. See the deepening relationship to yourself, becoming your own best friend. See your relationship to faith in Spirit grow as you realize that you are being lovingly guided each day.... Phase 7: Illumination...see your Self sitting peacefully in the sun, in the ecstatic silence of Pure Consciousness, Enlightened, like Christ or Buddha. You *observe* the body that houses your Self as you observe all of creation, with compassion and a deep understanding that there is no Enlightened place to get to and that there never has been. This peaceful state has always been here, simply awaiting your recall and awareness. There is only the being here, right now, in the sun....

Gently bringing this inward journey to a close, focus again on your breath... Slowly open your eyes and when you are ready, sit up. Spend some time writing about your experience of the journey. You may want to consider the following questions for yourself:

  a. Did you find yourself engaged or attached to one phase more than the others? If yes, which one?

  b. What did you experience emotionally? Physically? Mentally? Spiritually?

  c. Did certain aspects or events in your life have more of a charge for you? If yes, what were they?

d. Were you able to observe your life in fluid movement through the phases or did you experience yourself getting caught and emotionally stirred up? Gently take in your surroundings before you stand up and go about the rest of your day.

An Affirmation to Support
Your Journey Through the Seven Phases

"My life is in perfect order. I trust that I am being lovingly guided through each phase as I journey home to the truth of who I am."

5

Phase 1: Sleepwalking

"Your task is not to seek for love,
but merely to seek and find
all the barriers within yourself
that you have built against it."

—JALAL-AL-DIN RUMI

1. THE TRAUMA AND THE WOUND

Rick was an artist from a poor part of Trenton, New Jersey. His mother died when he was ten months old and his father, a drug addict, was emotionally and physically abusive to Rick. When Rick was as young as two years of age, his father would hit him and lock him in the apartment alone at night so he could go out to find drugs. He would tell him that he should have died instead of his mother. Rick coped by making TV his childhood friend. As an adult, Rick was quick to anger. He suffered many physical injuries, mostly due to car accidents. He would state his opinions but would not discuss them. He believed he was right, and he could not imagine another viewpoint. He had a big heart, but his ability to express his love was limited. He had tremendous fear of vulnerability. He resorted to rage instead. This was his way of protecting himself against opening and being emotionally available. He never considered seeking professional help for the abuse he had experienced. He was a sleepwalker.

In the Sleepwalking Phase, *your life is reactive, redundant, and unconscious.* Life is a surface experience, *without inquiry.* There is only one right, and it is held by the view of the sleepwalker. Being right is used as a protective shield against deeper thought and feelings. The pain of one's childhood is not addressed and thus gets projected onto others and out across the landscape of one's life. Somebody or something else is always responsible when situations and events don't go favorably for them. Unconsciously they feel powerless, but they tend to speak as if they believe, "I'm right and therefore powerful, even though the rest of the world doesn't understand me."

There is *no physical/body awareness of their emotional pain, nor awareness of the origins of that emotional pain.* Folks who live their life in this phase, are typically not open to healing and do not seek help. Mend a broken leg, yes, but uncover the reasons for the chronic dissatisfaction of their lives? No. For them to move out of this phase would require a Herculean effort. It is important to note that while this phase is unconscious, it holds the buried treasure of the true Self.

I was sleepwalking in my mid-twenties. I was seriously hurting (emotionally, mentally, physically, and spiritually,) and I had absolutely no clue that I had the power within me to change that. I took my distress as a condition of life.

It took four years of a life-threatening illness to shake me up, open my eyes, and set me searching for a deeper truth inside me.

Rick experienced the schizoid wounding outlined in Chapter 2. His trauma occurred soon after birth. His father hated having a child and resented having to care for him on his own. Rick had the added shock of the sudden loss of his mother. At such early ages the trauma is *a felt experience*, not a cognitive one. Rick was born into a hostile environment that said loud and clear that "he was not wanted." He carried this wound within him, acting it out with fits of rage and righteousness. He never attempted to heal it.

2. THE NEGATIVE MESSAGES

From the beginning, Rick got the strong message from his father that he was bad. He was a very intelligent child with a lot of physical energy. His father would try to repress his natural enthusiasm. When Rick was three, his father left him each day with a woman who kept Rick on a barricaded porch in all kinds of weather. He did not have toys, food, or adequate clothing. I asked him what he remembered from that experience. He said he remembered being cold, hungry, and bored. As he grew older, he would act out his aggression in the neighborhood with fights and wild antics. His neighbors called him "The Wild One" as he unconsciously released his anger through his rage. He grew up with the negative societal messages that he was poor and ignorant, and that he could never be educated or wealthy.

Rick dropped out of high school, learned a trade, and always struggled to make ends meet. He had several children. One day as they drove past a BMW dealership, his oldest son told him that he was going to buy a BMW when he grew up. Rick snickered and said, "In your dreams." As a sleepwalker, it *never occurred to Rick to question the negative messages he had received*. Without thinking, he passed those negative messages on to his children.

In my twenties, the message I received was that I was sad and depressing to be around. As a sleepwalker, I did not even consider the possibility that something might be going on inside of me to cause these feelings and that *those feelings were not who I am, but rather an expression of what I was feeling*. It wasn't until later that I discovered much of what I had been feeling was the result of massive hormonal disruptions from the illness, my distress about being so ill and from the unexplored pain of my wound.

AND THE NEGATIVE BELIEFS

From the negative messages he had received, Rick formed some very strong negative beliefs about himself and the world. He fervently believed that the world was unsafe. This was his earliest childhood experience, and growing up in a rough neighborhood "confirmed" that belief for him. Consequently, he was suspicious of almost everyone and everything. Unless they shared his worldview, Rick would not trust them. He would speak unkindly about most people out of the belief that they intended to hurt him. One evening, he and his friends drove past a young girl who appeared to be disoriented. His friends wanted to stop and help her, but Rick insisted that she was probably trying to trick them into stopping so she could rob them. He continued to drive on, refusing to help her. Again, the world for him was black and white, right or wrong. He could not conceive that someone might hold another view as valid as his.

Sadly, there are many people who live their lives asleep. When viewed from the perspective of negative beliefs, you need look no further than prejudice to find those who, to some degree, live without questioning. This can show up as distrust, hatred, and prejudgment of others because of gender, skin color, sexual preference, education, religious beliefs, financial status, ethnic backgrounds, countries, languages, and so on. Beyond the scope of humanity, there are prejudicial views toward certain species such as snakes, spiders, certain plants—the list is endless. Beyond that, there is prejudice toward technology and "other worlds," such as planets, galaxies, dimensions, and states of consciousness. The list of prejudices goes on and on. *Anything that draws a sharp line of bias in your mind and closes your heart holds the vibration of sleep.*

I accepted the messages that I was sad and depressed as the truth. I believed they were the definition of ME. Later, once I started to do the work of remembering the truth, I traced those beliefs back through a stream of messages I had received at various times in my life.

3. THE DEFENSE SYSTEMS AND JUDGING

As I wrote in Chapter 2, defense systems are natural to all life forms. The problem is that we tend to live our lives according to them, even when there is nothing to defend against. With sleepwalkers, *defenses are a chronic and essential part of daily life. They help to maintain the state of sleep.* They are never questioned.

Rick believed he had a whole unsafe world to defend against. He had a huge fascination with knives and swords. He had lots of them. As a young boy, carrying a knife was part of the standard dress code for survival in his neighborhood. As an adult, no matter where he lived, he carried that same belief and fear. Therefore, a knife was always in his back pocket. Whenever someone approached him, he was immediately suspicious. It did not occur to him that someone might just be saying hello.

Since everyone was unsafe, everyone was a potential enemy until Rick had a chance to get to know them. Thus, he would judge people constantly as a way to keep his distance and avoid real intimacy. Life without questioning is the safest way to stay fearful and separate. Fear and separation are essential to staying asleep.

Defense systems are not just physical things like knives. They are energetic, instinctual, and automatic. One person might puff their body up when defending, while another might silently collapse inward. Looking at the natural world is a great way to begin observing defenses. Just watch a cat or dog and see what they do when they feel threatened or unsafe. With Sleepwalking, however, defending becomes an unquestioned habit.

The defense I used in my twenties that kept me "safe" and asleep was withdrawal and isolation. If I was alone, then I did not have to deal with people believing I was depressing and no fun. I also did not have to question my choices, defenses, and deeper feelings that I was avoiding.

4. BELIEVING YOUR STORY IS ALL THERE IS

We all have stories. They are the history, the memories of our lives. The traumas and emotional wounds we experienced heavily script our unresolved stories. And then there are the stories we make up each day of our lives, interpreting and projecting our beliefs on to our life experiences. *In the Sleepwalking Phase, your history is the only reality,* and you become imprisoned by it. What happened in the past rules the present. With that belief, there is no point of changing; in fact, it seems like there is no possibility of change. In sleepwalking, people are very attached to their stories, and they talk about the same story repeatedly and without inquiry, which further cements it as reality.

Rick would often talk about the events of his life as if they were scripted and set in stone. He expected the story to repeat itself, and so it did. He would react to or avoid the circumstances of his life as the story played itself out. Believing your story is like burying your head in sand. From my experience, *we can use our stories as transformational tools to help us wake up and remember the truth of who we are.* We have freewill. So, we get to choose: Story as reality or story as a transformational tool. It's your story, your choice.

(Pause for a moment and consider: Which do you choose? Your story as the absolute reality or your story as a transformational tool?)

In my twenties, I believed my story was all there was. I was ill and suffering, and I could not imagine that my life could be different. After numerous times of being in and out of hospitals, in and out of surgeries, I believed that was going to be the story of my life. Little did I know that one year later, I would begin to challenge my story. It was only through questioning my story that my life began to change.

5. BELIEVING YOUR THOUGHTS

Thoughts precede emotions. What we think we feel, what we feel we transmit, and what we transmit we attract.

Rick completely believed every thought he had. He believed that if his mind thought that someone was out to get him, then it had to be true. He did not question his thinking process. For example, he could not even imagine that his fear-filled thoughts might be self-created and that he was projecting them onto someone else. Rick walked through life controlled by and powerless to his own thoughts, which were mostly fearful and negative. Consequently, he walked around feeling negative about life. Most people around him felt that negativity. While he had a few loyal friends, most of his friendships were superficial. Through his fear of connection and intimacy, he had created a lonely life, cut off from deep, nourishing relationships.

SLEEPWALKING IN CONCLUSION

Every phase of life has its purpose. The intention of this book is not to judge the various phases. It is to inspire you to delve into your life and explore the different phases within yourself. As I wrote in Chapter 4, these phases are not linear in their expression. At times, I momentarily go back to sleep. The difference between now and my mid-twenties is that I easily become aware that I have gone back to sleep. I then ask myself why and do the work to wake up again. As you progress, the tendency to sleepwalk diminishes, and the amount of time you go back to sleep decreases.

Sleepwalking is the easiest way to avoid being fully alive. When you realize that you are asleep or that you have gone back to sleep, and if you have the courage to ask yourself why, you will be led into a deeper, more compassionate understanding. *Just the act of questioning helps to wake you up again.* Second to that is forgiveness. Sometimes we just want to be Dorothy and lie down in the poppy fields and sleep, forget the pain, and forget the work of awakening. It's okay. Forgive yourself and you will be back on your way to remembering the truth of who you are.

One of the purposes of sleepwalking is the contrast in your perspective and the resulting positive actions when you begin to wake up. John Newton, the author of the song *Amazing Grace*, exemplifies this. He was a slaver who eventually realized the horrors of slave trading. It was after waking up that he began to support the abolitionist movement in England while going on to write one of the world's most beloved songs.

Finally, it is significant to note that *you can be awake in one area of your life and asleep in another.* Eventually, through doing the work of remembering, all the different areas of your life will awaken. Until then, it is useful to be reflective on the parts of your life where you are open, as well the parts of your life where you find yourself closed. Again, *inquiry* into all parts of yourself and your life will light the way, showing you the transformational work that awaits your attention.

CHAPTER #5

The Key Points to Sleepwalking

1. Sleepwalkers believe that life is happening to them, not with them. In other words, the Sleepwalker does not feel any responsibility for their life.
2. Life is lived on the surface of experience, without inquiry.
3. The sleepwalker's approach to life is reactive, redundant, and unconscious.
4. A sleepwalker believes that their opinions and beliefs are the only possible right ones.
5. Life is seen dualistically, right or wrong, good or bad.
6. There is no physical/body awareness of and connection to your emotional pain and its origin (your early childhood trauma and wound).
7. Anything that draws a sharp line in your mind and closes your heart holds the vibration of sleep.
8. In sleepwalking, your defense systems are an essential part of daily life. Defensive behaviors are not even considered as protective measures against deeper thought and feelings.

9. Your story, or history, is the only reality in the Sleepwalking Phase.

10. Sleepwalkers believe every thought that arises in their mind, without question.

11. Sleepwalking is the easiest way to avoid being fully alive.

12. The belief in a fear-induced sense of separation is essential to staying asleep.

13. Sometimes, you can be asleep in one area of your life and awake in another.

14. The true self is held as the buried treasure in this phase. It is awaiting discovery in the future phases of consciousness.

15. Inquiry helps to wake you up! Forgiveness does, too!

THE LIVING PRACTICE #5
Sleepwalking

Creating, Experiencing, Pause, Inquiry, and Transformation

Where Are You Sleepwalking in Your Life?

Find a quiet place for contemplation while considering the following:

1. Are there are parts of your life where you quickly judge things or events as right or wrong or good or bad? For example, I used to automatically judge my body as good (at a certain weight) or bad (at another weight).

2. Do you find yourself unwilling or unable to listen to another person's point of view about an issue or subject? If yes, do you know why?

3. How often do you experience yourself in defense? Begin observing yourself daily to see how often you automatically defend. For example, when angry, are you able to feel your heart area become tight and closed?

4. How has sleepwalking served you in your life?

5. What parts of your life story do you absolutely believe as the ultimate reality? For example, when I was going through my divorce, my ex-husband's family was angry with me because I had failed to get him sober. I believed the story that it was absolutely my responsibility to get him sober and that I was a failure since I had been unable to do that.

6. When you experience emotions, are you unable to also feel the body sensations that correlate to them? For example, when you feel love, are you able to feel the area in your chest where your physical heart is opening and soft? Or when you are angry, are you able to feel that same part of your body get tight and hard?

Inward Journey to Awaken from Sleepwalking
Find a comfortable place to lie down. Close your eyes and focus on your breathing, simply noticing the state of your breathing... You might discover that your breath is shallow or fast or anxious or deep or quiet. After discovering the quality of your breathing, take three long, slow, deep breaths with the intention to open and relax your body and your mind.... If you are already relaxed, this will support you dropping even deeper into an opened state of awareness.

Now imagine that you are going through your day just living on the surface of things, reacting to events and people. You get up, go to work, buy groceries, feed the kids, pay the bills, whatever activities comprise a typical day for you. Notice that as you go through your day you do not give any attention to what you might be feeling, needing, or longing... You don't really see the people around you. You just do what you must do, closed off from any deep connection to yourself or anyone else. You find yourself believing all your thoughts as they arise. You notice that most of your thoughts are negative, constantly judging events and people around you, dismissing people, dismissing life... You realize in this moment that you are sleepwalking. Your life feels like it's happening *to you, not with you*. You feel powerless to redirect it toward a path that would be meaningful.

Suddenly, you remember and feel from your childhood the bright vision and hopeful dreams that you had for yourself and your life.... Perhaps it was to sail the high seas or to write the next great novel, to care for animals, to be a brilliant mathematician or to learn to love deeply. Whatever it was—the pure, creative impulse in childhood, open to life and all its possibilities—feel it now. Feel the alive and joyful current of excitement and adventure coursing through your body, your emotions, and your mind.... See yourself waking up from a deep sleep of forgetting.

Feel yourself shedding fatigue, resignation, or despair as

easily as you would remove an outer coat.... Feel the freedom as you embody again the renewal and hope for an awakened and fulfilled life. Anchor this awareness in you by taking the time right now to connect it into the center of your beautiful heart... Plant it in your heart, so that it has a place to grow and blossom... It is yours, and it will help you on your journey as you move through the seven phases. Even though there may be much work between recalling your childhood wonder and manifesting it, the first step is evoking the memory of it and feeling it deeply.

Gently bringing this journey to a close, focus again on your breath. Slowly open your eyes, and when you are ready, sit up. Spend some time writing about your experience of the journey. You may want to consider the following questions:

   a. What did it feel like to experience yourself Sleepwalking through your life?

   b. Was anything familiar? If yes, what?

   c. Was anything comfortable or uncomfortable about Sleepwalking? If yes, what?

   d. Did you recall any childhood dreams that you had envisioned for your life? If yes, what were they? If yes, what did you feel emotionally and physically as you remembered them?

e. Have any of those dreams been fulfilled? If yes, which ones? If not, consider why they have not been fulfilled. If some have been realized and others are still waiting to manifest, consider what might be in the way of manifesting them and write about that.

f. If you did not recall any childhood dreams, take some time to write about how this feels and what it means for you.

g. Take some more time to write down any dreams (either from childhood or new ones) that you may want to pursue in your life from this moment forward.

Gently take in your surroundings before you stand up and go about the rest of your day.

An Affirmation to Support You in the Areas of Yourself and Your Life

Where You Might be Sleepwalking

"I understand that each phase, even sleepwalking, has a spiritual purpose. I trust that Spirit, in perfect timing, will lovingly help me to awaken all the parts of myself that are asleep, helping me to remember the truth of who I am."

6

PHASE 2: DENIAL

"Most men would rather deny a hard truth than face it."

—GEORGE R.R. MARTIN,
A Game of Thrones

1. THE TRAUMA AND THE WOUND

Mary's flaming red hair always turned heads. Though she was from Brooklyn, her neighbors had fondly called her "Ireland." She came from a working-class background. Her father, who was of Irish descent, never finished high school but always held a good job and provided for his family. Mary had two brothers, both younger than she. Her strictly Protestant family spent a great deal of time observing religious rituals. Mary had a special relationship with her father. He was kind to her, and they were close. On the other hand, her mother doted on her brothers and constantly criticized Mary. Her mother was a tough woman of few emotions. She ruled the family. She had placed such a tremendous focus on appearance and cleanliness that each child developed obsessive-compulsive tendencies around physical order and cleanliness. Mary shared with me that as a child she felt alternately controlled (the Masochistic wound) and abandoned (the Oral wound) by her mother. As a child, this had left her feeling sad. As an adult, Mary would deny this sadness, saying, "I had good parents. They loved me."

Root of Denial

Denial prevents us from living honestly. It diminishes our capacity to experience the full range of emotions. It deters our ability to question what is working and not working in our lives. We live in denial when we need or want to avoid issues and feelings. The origin of denial begins in childhood when certain life experiences were just too much for us to process and integrate. Instead we repressed them by denying them. As adults, we continue to deny in order to avoid processing, integrating, and growing from both past and current life experiences. Dysfunctional family systems often encourage denial as a strategy to avoid painful issues.

Denial arises out of 100%, right/wrong thinking. This is the thinking of child-consciousness. There is no room for 50%-50% thinking. In other words, in Mary's mind there was no way she could have emotional pain about her childhood *and* have parents who loved her. Subsequently, she has had to deny her unhappiness so that she can acknowledge the love she did receive. In the child-consciousness mind, if Mary were to acknowledge her pain, she would have to conclude that her parents did not love her. Only if she came out of denial could she accept both as true. In reality, Mary was loved and she also has unresolved emotional pain.

Another element of denial is the *abandonment of self*. Mary abandoned her own self by denying her pain, her right to be sad. She controlled her feelings by denying them and instead would pretend she was never angry, upset, or sad. If someone suggested that she was angry, she would vehemently deny it. And yet, she walked around acting as if each day was a burden, something to be endured. She focused on cleanliness, her appearance, her never-ending daily tasks, and a masked behavior of kindness rather than going deeply into her inner world and feelings.

When I was in my early thirties, I had a short and disastrous marriage to a man who was an alcoholic. One of the times he was in recovery, his counselor suggested that I go to Al-Anon (a program for friends and families of Alcoholics). He said he could see that I was angry. I was indignant. I asked him why I should have to go to Al-Anon. After all, I wasn't the one with the problem. My husband was the alcoholic. I assured him that my anger would go away as soon as my husband got well. I was denying my anger and sadness about being in a painful marriage and about being unable to control my husband's disease. I was denying my codependency. I was also denying my anger about some of my life choices and my own earlier experiences about being helpless. I was projecting my anger onto my husband's disease. Months later, when I finally showed up at an Al-Anon meeting, I began to realize the unspoken influence alcoholism had played in my own family. I learned that the whole family takes part in the denial of the disease. This had certainly been true in my father's family. As I started to trace back, I discovered that my paternal grandfather and great-grandfather had been alcoholics. My father later shared with me that two of his great-uncles had committed suicide under the influence of alcohol.

(Pause for a moment to consider:
Is there something you might be in denial about?
If yes, what is it? How does this feel?)

2. THE NEGATIVE MESSAGES

The negative messages we received and our belief in them play a powerful role in denial. Because negative messages are so damaging, we tend to deny them and the painful feelings connected to them. It's as if someone says you are stupid and you deny that someone even said that. You may deny how you feel about them for saying that or deny your feelings about being told you are stupid. When I was in Junior High School I endured painful bullying by a group of girls, one of whom had been my best friend in 6th grade. Seventh grade had brought on a growth spurt for me, and suddenly I was about five inches taller than they were. That was enough for them to decide to dislike me. Yet despite their sneers and not letting me join them for lunch in the cafeteria, I still pretended we were friends. We would go to the mall together and they would run away from me and hide. I could hear them giggling and making fun of me. I would pretend they weren't being cruel, and when they finally came out of hiding I would pretend they hadn't left me. I had no place to put my feelings at that age, so I denied them. I pretended everything was okay with these girls, even though deep inside of me I felt a sense of despair. *Denial is a way of protection*. Unfortunately, the protection it offers also deters honesty and growth.

Parental Messages

Mary had a minor deformity in her right hand. That, along with a constant level of anxiety of not being good enough, undermined her self-esteem. As a child, she did not receive the medical support that could have easily resolved the deformity. Instead, she got a negative parental message from her mother that something was wrong with her. As an adult, she carried a lot of shame about this. She would say that the issue with her right hand was because she hadn't been good enough as a child. In saying this, she denied the fact that she had a physical issue that had never been addressed.

Self-Generated Messages

Mary's low self-esteem led her to give many negative messages to herself despite her apparent physical beauty. She rarely said anything positive about her appearance. Instead, she would constantly ask questions like, "Is my makeup okay, what about my outfit, my hair?" Before anyone could confirm her, she would answer herself, "I know I don't look good."

Mary would get the roots of her hair dyed every few weeks. One time I asked her about it. She replied, "My roots are the only part of my hair that grays, the rest is red." I started to explain to her that all her hair would be gray if she did not dye the roots. Then I realized that Mary's red hair was the only physical attribute she felt somewhat good about. Otherwise, she hated her looks and worried about aging. As long as she could deny that all her hair would be gray, she was able to hold on to some sense of being physically attractive and youthful. That is how strong denial lives in her.

Societal Messages

Mary's religious background was strict. The message she received over and over is that when good things happened to her, God loved her. When bad things happened, it was because God was disappointed in her, and that she was bad and had to do penance. Literally everything that happened to her was because she was either being favored by God or reprimanded by God. She walked around with a sad face and a lot of shame, with the sense that she was defective at her core. She would rarely make eye contact. She was very self-conscious, and she avoided direct social interactions as much as possible.

Denial is a means of avoidance. Unlike the Sleepwalker who is unaware about what is going on beneath the surface of things, the person in denial feels discomfort, pain, and unrest about the looming issues, but avoids dealing with them.

"Now what state do you live in? Denial."
—Bill Watterson, *The Essential Calvin and Hobbes: A Calvin and Hobbes Treasury*

Denial is a tool for deflection. During sessions, Mary often complained about her job and how tired she was. She never took off more than one day at a time and spoke poorly of those who took off a week or more. Even though she suffered from working so much, she did not want to consider the reasons for denying herself. When I asked her why she didn't take more time for herself, she would deflect the question by saying things like, "Oh I will when it slows down." (It never did.)

Denial is linked to shame. In other words, shame helps keep denial in place. As long as Mary was focused on her shame and embarrassment about her hand, she could deny her true feelings about it.

"You will never find the real truth among people that are insecure or have egos to protect. Truth over time becomes either guarded or twisted as their perspective changes; it changes with the seasons of their shame, love, hope or pride." —Shannon L. Alder

As my ex-husband's drinking increased, my shame about my situation increased and, subsequently, my denial got stronger. I started to refuse invitations to social events, feigning headaches and work. I started to avoid conversations with neighbors, and when we did talk it was only about the weather, never about the loud fight that had gone on in my house the night before. I felt so much shame about myself and my marriage that I denied the deep grief and anger inside of me. Instead, I focused on my husband's alcoholism and behavior, not the underlying issues of my own codependency.

AND THE NEGATIVE BELIEFS

Negative beliefs often arise out of the negative messages or out of painful life experiences. Denial encourages us to hold on to our negative beliefs, rather than to question and heal them.

Mary experienced the sudden and tragic loss of her first husband when she was nineteen. She never received emotional support for her loss. Instead, she was told to be strong, and that meant to not ask for help. There was a belief passed on to her by her parents that strong people buckle up, pray, and move on. But Mary could not move on.

She became depressed and socially withdrew. Still, no one thought to intervene. In the ensuing years, she had a boyfriend who died in a car accident. Mary believed that she was bad luck to be with, and since that time never committed to a relationship. She drifted from man to man, occasionally having affairs with married men. Mary had a strong negative belief that she was bad luck, and she would choose unavailable men to support that belief. Her denial about the huge losses she had experienced drove her into isolation so that she would not have to deal with her feelings and negative beliefs. In denial, *our negative beliefs act as a means to control and thwart introspection and forward movement.*

One day, after his first round in a recovery program, my husband and I were out driving. Every time we drove by a bar or a liquor store he would fixate on the place. I remember being completely baffled by his behavior. I would ask myself, "Why is he looking at those places? He doesn't drink anymore." Boy, did I have a lot to learn, and yes, I was in denial! His family, who lived in perpetual denial about his illness as well as other family problems, thought I was his savior and that I would heal him. I believed that was my job. Since childhood, I had carried a negative belief that it was my job to make sure everyone was okay. When I failed at "healing" him of his alcoholism, his family turned on me. That sense of failure, coupled with my childhood experience of not being able to make everyone around me happy, evoked the negative belief in myself that whatever I did, it was not enough and that meant I was not good enough. Along with that I held the belief that I was a failure. In denial, there is the avoidance of dealing with the deep feelings and negative beliefs by focusing on behavior and actions. For me, focusing on healing my husband helped me to avoid confronting my own negative beliefs.

3. THE DEFENSE SYSTEMS AND JUDGING

The initial purpose of defense systems is that they are designed to protect. An activated defense system is an automatic reaction to any perceived threat. That threat can be anything from real harm to something that is perceived as a potential threat to your sense of self. In *denial, your sense of self is so hidden that the threat could be the possibility of genuinely feeling emotions or becoming aware of the issue at hand.*

Denial is a great defense. It creates a force field that says, "Do not enter." Remember, Sleepwalkers *live* in defense.

For them it's just a steady, unconscious rhythm. For those in denial however, defenses are used liked Ping-Pong/table tennis. As soon as the truth comes toward them (they sense the truth is coming) they will send the truth back by denying it. There is also a tremendous amount of judging in denial. Much like Ping-Pong, *judging the self and judging others is a very effective way of staying closed and in denial.* Once, after an unsuccessful attempt to question Mary's defense of deflection, I asked her if she had any thoughts about denial. She surprised me when she quickly answered, "Oh, I am in denial about a lot of things."

Sometimes, shocking events in your life evoke denial as a way of self-preservation. Years ago, my beloved dog Jessie was hit by a car and killed ten minutes before I reached home. My friend Jane had put Jessie in the car and was ready to take her to the veterinarian to see if she was alive. I got home just as her car was backing out of the driveway. Jane was in shock and in denial. I opened the back end of her car and saw Jessie lying there lifeless. I wanted to believe that she was alive by going into denial as well, but I knew she was gone. Jane kept insisting that perhaps something could be done. I knew it was her way of not wanting to feel the pain. I, too, did not want to feel my heartbreak, but there it was, crumbling inside of me. I just could not deny it, and the tears started to flow.

4. BELIEVING YOUR STORY IS ALL THERE IS

Denial is part of forgetting. It is a self-imposed amnesia. For Mary, believing her story that "Since my parents loved me, they could do no wrong, death follows me, when good fortune happens God is saying he loves me, when bad things happen to me God is saying he doesn't approve and I've done something wrong" leaves her no opening for inquiry and healing. Denial is like a very high fence. You may know the fence is there, but you dare not investigate what is on the other side for fear that what you might find may require you to see what you've been avoiding, and to question and change.

Humanity fills the world with stories. We have our individual stories and our collective stories. Families and groups, as well as individuals, may use denial in their stories as a means of not dealing with issues. In denial, if we keep telling ourselves a story and believing it, we don't have to deal with it.

Years ago, I took a course that shared the same title as the required text, *Crimes Against Humanity*. One section of the book focused on international law and the terms of the Geneva Convention. One international law requires countries to report acts of genocide as crimes against humanity. Author Geoffrey Robertson QC writes that in January of 1994, as the Rwandan genocide was beginning, there was direct intelligence between the British and the Americans that genocide was imminent. However, because both countries did not want to get involved, they refused to use the word genocide, knowing that by doing so they would be required to act under the Geneva Convention. Robertson inferred that the Clinton Administration and the British Foreign Office devised a story that it was "tribal hatred," blacks killing blacks, and therefore was not genocide. Their position suggested that tribal people and/or people of the same race killing one another negate the possibility of genocide. It's sort of like the movie *Wag the Dog*, directed by Barry Levinson. Make up a story, believe it, and convince others to believe it as a means of *denying what is really happening*. Some years later in an ABC News article dated February 28, 2014, journalist Dana Hughes wrote, "President Clinton has called the failure to intervene in

Rwanda one of his biggest regrets." When we come out of denial we see that we created stories to support our denial. We are then free to acknowledge the truth.

Sometimes it's easier to see it on a global level, but the same thing is happening with stories and denial on the individual level. As an example, I got a call a few weeks ago from a friend. He told me his ex-girlfriend had called him to share that she was having knee surgery. He had undergone knee surgery when they were together. She had vanished during his hospitalization and recovery. Her absence was "the straw that broke the camel's back," and he ended the relationship. Now, during her call to him, she asked him how his knee was doing. He replied, "Fine." She went on to tell him that she was happy she had been there for him during his surgery, commenting on how well she had taken care of him afterward. As he was telling me this he said, "I sat there listening to her weave this whole story about how she'd 'been there' for me. I knew it was really just for her, so that she could deny her pain at not being with me when I needed her, as well as allay her own fears about her upcoming surgery."

Another problem about denial as a psychological defense mechanism is that it can cause us to deny not only the negative experiences or issues, but also our happiness and good qualities. Remember, *denial is an avoidance strategy.* Pain can also arise from knowing there are beautiful parts of ourselves that have gone unrecognized or that are connected to issues we have chosen to ignore. Some time ago I had a boyfriend who loved me very much. He thought I was beautiful, and he would tell me so several times a day. That was the problem. Why? I have a younger sister who was a homecoming queen. During the homecoming parade, someone came up to me and asked, "How can you be her sister? She's so pretty." Those words cut deep into me and became part of a story that I believed about myself. So, when my boyfriend would say, "You're beautiful," I denied it. I did not believe him; perhaps I did not want to believe him. It was too risky to trust his words. It seemed safer to believe the story the stranger had said to me. That was the story I had taken to be true.

Mary also felt it was far safer for her to believe the stories she had both lived and constructed as a means of keeping herself small. As long as she was in denial, she did not have to make a conscious choice to change. Such an action would have meant not only opening to her pain but to the joy of living, as well.

Our stories, our memories, serve as tools to help us grow. But when we get trapped in negative stories about ourselves, which is what happens with denial, change and growth are not possible.

5. BELIEVING YOUR THOUGHTS

Most of us believe our thoughts. Most live without questioning them. While this is 100 percent true for sleepwalkers, it's about 98 percent true for those who live in denial. *Denial is so hard-wired that most of our thoughts are there to serve the denial.* There is little or no inquiry as to the validation or accuracy of your thoughts. And just as in sleepwalking, your thoughts lean to the negative spectrum, though with denial what comes out of your mouth might sound negative, or might sound like sugar. Either way is a toxic attempt to avoid being genuine and real. For Mary, the truth brewed right beneath her negative thoughts. It was for this reason that she would instinctively react to any query attempting to dip below the surface of her thoughts by instantly regurgitating a statement of denial.

Denial in Conclusion

Denial, in my view, is pandemic. To return to the truth

of who you are and live your full potential, you need to be willing to gently let go of denial and enter the world within you. You need to face uncomfortable truths. You need to feel them. The feelings that you have avoided have been coated with denial.

> *"The conflict between the will to deny*
> *horrible events and the will to proclaim them aloud*
> *is the central dialectic of psychological trauma."*
> —Judith Lewis Herman, *Trauma and Recovery*

In the next chapter, "SOS," we will explore the tipping point that opens the door to healing. You need to go inside. Your inner world awaits you with clues and guidance to help you remember the truth of who you are.

CHAPTER #6

The Key Points to Denial

1. Denial is a defense.
2. Denial can be a useful tool for protection and self-preservation until you are equipped to deal with a traumatic experience.
3. It is a way to ignore issues and emotions.
4. It is a way to avoid being genuine or real.
5. Denial deters our ability to question honestly what is working and not working in our lives.
6. Its origin is unresolved childhood traumas and wounds or current traumatic life experiences.
7. Denial pretends that nothing is wrong and avoids what is really happening, like "the elephant in the room" metaphor. Everyone knows there is a problem but no one wants to address it.
8. Denial is a way of protecting against experiencing pain, fear, or helplessness.
9. Unlike the sleepwalker who is unconscious, in denial we experience a degree of discomfort that we are choosing to avoid.
10. Denial is a tool for deflection.
11. Denial helps us hold on to our negative beliefs by

focusing on our own or someone else's outward behavior and actions.
12. Denial is a form of a control.
13. Judging the self or others helps to maintain denial.
14. Denial is part of forgetting. It is a self-imposed amnesia.
15. In denial, we are abandoning ourselves.
16. We will deny not only our pain but our right to happiness and our good qualities.

THE LIVING PRACTICE #6
Creating Kindness and Compassion for the Denial in Your Life

Creating, Experiencing, Pause, Inquiry, and Transformation

Find a quiet place for contemplation while considering the following:

1. I have yet to meet a person who has not been in denial about something. Remember, it is a defense to protect you from painful feelings and inquiry about yourself or certain life experiences. Take the time now to gently recall your life history. Choose one past event or situation that you previously were or may currently be in denial about. If you can't recall one for yourself, perhaps you can recall someone in your life whose denial about something affected you. Once you have identified the situation, event, or person, write about it in detail.

2. Once you feel complete in what you have written, I want you to put it down for an hour or so. When

you come back, I want you to take a few moments to connect with your heart and your capacity to love. Once you feel connected, I want you to read what you have written, not from the eyes of judging yourself or the other for being in denial, but through the eyes and heart of someone who has compassion. Were you able to do this? If yes, how did it feel? Have you experienced any internal shifts or any insights? If you were unable to feel compassion or connect with your heart, then write about that. Spirit is filled with compassion for you, no matter where you are in any given moment.

3. Now, make a list of how denial protected you or the other in the experience you wrote about. In other words, how did being in denial serve you and what have you learned from it? For example, denying my sadness and anger while the girls in seventh grade made fun of me helped me to have the courage to get on the bus and go to school. I learned so much about myself, and how I handle or deny pain. I learned why people deny bullying is happening to them or others and why people deny that they are bullies. What have you learned in this exercise about denial in you, in your life? Write about that.

4. Consider your current life. It takes great courage to

be honest with ourselves, and yet honesty holds the potential for great healing. Where in your current life are you in denial? How is your present denial serving you? Can you feel compassion for yourself? What can you give to yourself to help you to move out of denial? What kind of support do you need to do that?

Inward Journey to Become Compassionate and Kind with Denial

Find a comfortable place to lie down. Close your eyes and focus on your breathing, just noticing the state of your breathing... You might discover that your breath is shallow or fast or anxious or deep or quiet. After discovering the quality of your breathing, take a few long, slow, deep breaths with the intention to open and relax your body and your mind.... If you are already relaxed, this will support you dropping even deeper into an opened state of awareness.

For this inward journey, you are going to use the experience that you wrote about in the previous questions. Visualize yourself or the other in full denial, standing in front of you... As you look at yourself or them, notice if you have a demand that you or they come out of denial, that you or they become aware of whatever they are denying, that you or they do something to change their situation. Are you agitated, impatient, angry, interested, or empathic? Simply note your experience. As you look at yourself or them, notice if you have a demand that you or they come out of denial, that you or they become aware of whatever they are denying, that you or they do something to change to their situation. What do you feel physically and emotionally inside of your body while you are demanding?

Imagine there is a basket on the floor beside you. Whatever reactions you might be having about the person in denial (even if that person is you), I ask that for the moment, you place your reactions and demands in the basket. Take some time to do this... Now, free of reactions, I want you to look again at the person who is in denial. (Again, this person might be you.) With a clear intention, I want you to ask to be shown what is underneath the denial. You need to open your heart to see and feel that which they (or you) are avoiding. Perhaps it is fear or anger or grief or helplessness. Trust whatever your heart perceives.... Once you have perceived what they or you are protecting against, tell them or yourself that to the best of your ability you are willing to be compassionate and kind, whether they or you are in denial. Let yourself feel the truth of your compassion in your heart... See them look at you with trust as you receive you or them just as they are. You feel yourself or them fading in front of you as they thank you for your kindness.

Gently bringing this journey to a close, focus again on your breath. Slowly open your eyes, and when you are ready, sit up. Spend some time writing about your experience of the journey. You may want to consider the following questions:

a. What did it feel like to judge and demand that you or the other in denial change, for you to feel okay?

b. What did it feel like to see/feel their or your pain underneath the denial?

c. If you were able, what did it feel like to open your heart and experience compassion, understanding, and kindness toward yourself or them?

Gently take in your surroundings before you stand up and go about the rest of your day.

An Affirmation to Support You in the Areas of Yourself and Your Life Where You Might Be in Denial

"I release any judgment or demands that I may hold toward myself about denial. I trust that Spirit will gently help me heal the places of denial inside of me in perfect timing."

7

PHASE 3: SOS (HELP! CRISIS!)

"You had to break, to be unbroken.
In the brokenness, I had found
that which was unbroken.
That which was perfect,
and beautiful, and complete."

—T. SCOTT McLEOD,
The Light in the Darkness

1. THE TRAUMA AND THE WOUND

Marco came to me, as he said, "a broken man." He was European, at the top of his career in international real estate, divorced, angry, and alone. A chain smoker, and not allowed to smoke in session, he would sit in his chair spewing angry words about an angry world. He shared that the only reason he had made an appointment with me was because he was desperate. He was outwardly successful, but inwardly he felt like a failure. He alternated between feeling hollow or filled with rage. He felt adrift, without purpose.

In our beginning sessions, I asked him about his childhood. I knew the intense feelings in him were not new. He shared that his father was cold and strict. At home, discussion about any issue was unthinkable. His father was always right, and Marco was forced to obey. His father also used Marco to fulfill his own unrealized religious goals with the church. Marco talked about his Catholic education and the nuns who, for the most part, were as strict as his father. As a child, he had no refuge. With no safe place to go, he buried his feelings. Now, ready to explode, he had made an appointment. He had signaled SOS, the call of distress, for help, crisis.

SOS is a powerful phase. It is like standing in front of a dam that is holding back as much water as is possible and a storm is coming. In SOS, you find yourself at the tipping point, and you are highly motivated *to release the floodgates of feelings* that have been held back by sleepwalking and denial. You may not be consciously aware of this, but *at the soul level you are finally ready to heal.*

SOS is not to be taken lightly. I remember when I went to my second Al-Anon meeting. I was wild-eyed, confused, and utterly lost. I had no idea as to any sense of direction in my life. I did not even know at the time if Al-Anon was right for me. Frankly, I was just trying to stay alive. All I knew was that my level of suffering had become intolerable and that I would try any type of therapy or support to be out of pain. During that meeting, I was struck by the practical wisdom of a woman thirty years my senior. In Al-Anon they suggest you get a "sponsor," someone in the program who can help mentor you through the twelve steps. I went up to her after the meeting and asked if she would be my sponsor. She looked me directly in the eyes and said, "Yes, but I'm no babysitter." Her words shocked me. In hindsight, I realized that her frankness had helped to shake me out of the stupor of sleepwalking and denial. Her words had sparked the thought that perhaps *the power to change was inside of me.* SOS is the wakeup call. It is the time when the self says, loud and clear, "I am ready to change."

2. THE NEGATIVE MESSAGES YOU RECEIVED

Parental Messages

While Marco's father was strict, his mother was timid. His father would order his mother and him around, and if Marco began to protest, his father would hit him. His mother did nothing to stop his father, but she would go to Marco afterward for solace. This conveyed several messages to Marco.

One of those was that he was guilty and he deserved to be punished. The second was that men are in charge. He witnessed his mother's fear time and again when his father would set out to punish him. Marco shared with me that as an adult he would order his girlfriends around. If they disagreed or disobeyed him, he would leave them.

Societal Messages

Marco's education and religion were both in the Catholic Church. The nuns delivered the same message as his father: He was guilty, and he deserved to be punished. He spoke of being in church, seeing the image of Christ nailed to the cross, and being told that Christ had died for his sins. He remembered being repeatedly told that he would go to hell if he did not obey his father, the nuns, and the church.

Self-Generated Messages

Given the recurring messages from his father, his mother, and the church, it was easy for Marco to create self-generated messages of hatred. When he started working with me, he had so much self-hatred that he could not even begin to see himself clearly.

This is an important point about SOS—*nothing is clear but the eruption of pain*. It is not yet time for knowledge and understanding, nor is it the time for the deep integrative work of release. It is the time to begin to be cognizant of the confusion that has been created by messages based on distortion and fear. This period of uncertainty evokes an "identity crisis." I tell my students that this is an essential point on the path of remembering the truth of who you are. I call it the "being lost" time. Here's the good news: *You know you're lost!* In sleepwalking and denial, you don't know you are lost. There is no hesitation, no awareness of how far away from the true self you have strayed, no questioning. You're just "going with the program." *When you are signaling SOS, you feel the disorientation. You begin to question*, "Who am I? Is the way I have been living, in so much pain, the only way for me? Is life supposed to be about suffering and misery? Am I supposed to feel bad about myself? Is there another way?" While painful, these questions are the points of light that will begin to illuminate the way of healing in you.

I remember feeling crazy when I could not get my ex-husband sober. A message I had given myself as a teenager was that it was my job to fix the issues my parents might be having in their marriage and that I was supposed to ensure peace and happiness. My ex-husband's family confirmed the message and my identity as the "fixer." They told me it was my job to get him sober. And I really tried. At one point, we separated. During that time my ex-husband attempted suicide, and he ended up being institutionalized. When I went to visit him, the number of heavily medicated patients who sat around, lost in a stupor, struck me. My ex-husband and I went for a walk. Since I was the one who had initiated the separation, I felt responsible for his attempted suicide. As we walked, we talked about living together again. He began making all of kinds of demands. Each time I agreed with one of his demands, he would change it and demand something different. *Finally*, a light bulb went on in me: *"He was the one"* in the psychiatric hospital, not me. I left the hospital and filed for a divorce. I could not fix him. I had reached the point of SOS. I did not know what to do or where to turn; I just knew that something was terribly wrong in the negative messages I had received and the identity I had taken on as a result. In that moment, I knew the only person I could fix or save was myself. Dear reader, the same holds true for you.

> *The Journey*
> One day you finally knew
> what you had to do, and began,
> though the voices around you
> kept shouting
> their bad advice—
> though the whole house
> began to tremble

and you felt the old tug

at your ankles.

"Mend my life!"

each voice cried.

But you didn't stop.

You knew what you had to do,

though the wind pried

with its stiff fingers

at the very foundations,

though their melancholy

was terrible.

It was already late

enough, and a wild night,

and the road full of fallen

branches and stones.

But little by little,

as you left their voices behind,

the stars began to burn

through the sheets of clouds,

and there was a new voice

which you slowly

recognized as your own,

that kept you company

> as you strode deeper and deeper
>
> into the world,
>
> determined to do
>
> the only thing you could do—
>
> determined to save
>
> the only life you could save.
>
> —Mary Oliver

And the Negative Beliefs

The negative messages we receive are the foundation for the negative beliefs we live by. Some of these beliefs are familial and run through generations. Some are culturally driven by race, religion, gender, politics, and so on. Still others are deeply rooted in our species and our current place on the evolutionary scale.

Marco had formed many negative beliefs. The one that underscored the rest, and the one he shares with much of humanity, is the belief that he is bad. His father's message and the message he received from the church left little room for doubt. Being used for comfort by his mother while being told by his father he was bad caused the Psychopathic wounding (outlined in chapter 2) in Marco.

When he had grown intolerably weary of being bad, Marco had reached the phase of SOS. The belief that he was bad had not brought him closer to his father, God, himself, or others. On the contrary, it had enforced a self-imposed isolation and a high degree of self-hatred. He believed that since he was bad, he was not fit to be around. When he reached the tipping point of SOS, he was *ready to question the negative beliefs* that had never offered him a way out of the torment of isolation and self-hatred. In our work together I assured Marco, "Change your beliefs and you change your reality." This gave him hope that perhaps he did have the power within himself to heal.

Coupled with *the rooted belief in humanity that "we are bad" is* the fearful belief that we are separate from the rest of creation and therefore very alone in our badness. Our negative beliefs lead to the cementing of our defense systems.

3. THE DEFENSE SYSTEMS AND JUDGING

Marco's defense system was to dominate his environment, his work, his feelings, and his significant relationships. Through domination no one could get too close to him, and he would not have to get close to his deep feelings of sadness and rage. That was until SOS, when he finally became fed up with his isolation. All the cigarettes in the world could no longer quell his rising anxiety, and he screamed inside of himself, "Help."

In our early work together, Marco pretty much stayed skeptical and defended. His defensive strategy during that time was to counter each suggestion I made to him. I understood this. I know that while *SOS is a powerful catalyst for change, it is also fragile.* It is important to remember that during SOS, you do not have the knowledge or the tools to navigate the healing process. While you are still in the dark, *you desperately want to believe that there really is light at the end of the tunnel.*

Patience is needed when dealing with defenses during SOS. Also essential during this time is the constant reflection of love back to the person in distress. Any challenge to the defense system during SOS can create greater confusion in the individual and may send them back into denial or sleep. *Gentle, gentle is the way.* This is also not the time for logic that is aimed to convince someone to drop his or her defenses. *SOS is deeply emotional.* Those in this phase need to be held with unconditional loving. Meeting them in this way helps to establish trust. Trust cultivates the determination necessary to take the next step into the Knowledge and Resources Phase.

I have experienced the SOS phase a few times in my life. Early on in my path of healing, there were a few powerful events spread over an eight-year period that catapulted me back into SOS, feeling blind and desperate as ever. *The lifelines that saved me came from the outside.* They came from the outside because in this phase there is just not enough recognition of the essential core self to guide us. The first lifeline was my first therapist, whom I credit to this day for saving my life. The second was the discipline of meditation that I held on to for dear life. The third were the communities of help and healing I found, Al-Anon being one of them. Again, this phase is desperate and emotional, we are stumbling, reaching out for someone, something to hold on to just to get through the day.

One of the reasons for both the power and fragility of SOS is that *our belief system about ourselves and life has been turned upside down.* During this phase, all the judging we have toward ourselves and others has started to crumble. Remember, judging is the Great Separator. In SOS, we need to do something different to be released from pain. Therefore, judging during this phase is often cast away, not out of wisdom, but out of desperation. Our beliefs and judgments are deeply embedded in our story. And in SOS, for the first time, we begin to question if the story of our life is really all there is.

4. BELIEVING YOUR STORY IS ALL THERE IS

I have witnessed a phenomenon time and again with my students and clients, and I have experienced it in my own life. Often, clients come only after they experience their lives falling apart. Lost and bewildered, they come looking for assurance and sanity. SOS is volatile in a very promising way. The dam has burst, and their life and story, which they had bought as the ultimate reality, is crumbling before them.

This is what brought Marco to me. He had bought the belief that he was bad. His life story had confirmed this over and over. When he slammed into the SOS Phase, desperate for help, his story wasn't making sense anymore. It was a huge challenge for Marco to consider the possibility that a reality beyond being bad might be possible for him. *The problem with our stories is that we are often encouraged to believe them.* They are also known and therefore safe. When we begin to question them, our reality gets shaken. Added to that are the stories that are expected of many of us. Grow up, get an education, get a job, get married, have children, get a mortgage, go on vacations, and retire someday. This is a typical Western story that many believe is the track they are supposed to follow.

But what do you do when that path eclipses you, or when you find yourself pulled in another direction? It can be very disorienting. It can also promote self-doubt and even despair. We are typically conditioned not to think and question for ourselves and, even more, many of us are conditioned not to take the risks to listen to and follow our deep heart's longing. For in conditioned society, the story is IT.

Marco had really tried to believe the story he had been told. But fortunately for him, the pain of self-betrayal became so great that it won out over the story. *It takes tremendous courage to challenge our stories.* I have told my students over the years that while *our stories are useful transformational tools,* they are not the ultimate reality.

I remember when I began to wake up from story. Part of my belief system and story was that romantic love was supposed to be difficult; it was supposed to be a struggle, and it was supposed to hurt. I had already witnessed this in my life. In my late teens, I fell in love with a wonderful man. He was kind, funny, and passionate, and we were inseparable. After we were together for some time, I felt the impact of my negative beliefs and my story. It was as if I heard, "Your love is too easy and therefore it can't be right." Eventually, I broke off the relationship, though it was very painful to do so. A long physical illness ensued. At the end of the illness, when I began to "wake up" about the incredible distortion that I had bought about love, I telephoned him. I told him I had made a mistake in leaving him and that I wanted to get back together. He said he never wanted to have to say this to me, but he was getting married. I was devastated. I have lived with the painful result of believing the story that love hurts. In fact, by leaving him, I had made my story a reality. It has taken many years of healing to let go of that story as *the* reality and to open again to the truth that love heals and that love is kind. I felt the SOS Phase in me as I felt the wild sorrow and pain of having left him. Lost, I sought help and then had to find my way back to myself. For Marco, too, once he called out for help, he was on his way. *SOS renders us open.*

5. BELIEVING YOUR THOUGHTS

The SOS Phase becomes interesting in a revolutionary "aha" way when you *begin feeling* the insanity of your negative thoughts/thinking.

As I shared earlier, an "aha" moment for me came while I was following my ex-husband around in the field as he spouted what I needed to do for our marriage. My thoughts were agreeing with his insanity. And in that moment, *I felt* the insanity of it all—my thoughts and his thoughts.

Marco also had believed his thoughts about himself, until he reached the SOS Phase. It was then that he began to question their validity. Our thinking (which often tends to the negative and is habitually repetitious) is a fierce obstacle.

The next movement along the path helps to provide insight into our thought processes. This is the Knowledge and Resources Phase. Here, we actively search for direction and guidance that will help light the path and steady the way. Come along as we go through that door.

CHAPTER #7

The Key Points to SOS (Help! Crisis!)

1. SOS is the turning point of beginning the work to remember the truth of who you are.
2. It is the wakeup call.
3. In SOS, nothing is clear but the eruption of pain. It is the long-held suppression and/or denial of emotional turmoil that has built up in you to this point.
4. You are experiencing an "identity crisis", a "dark night of the soul."
5. At the soul level, SOS means you are ready to heal.
6. Lifelines come from the outside in SOS. A steady reflection of love and confirmation of your ability to heal helps alleviate the acute distress you feel.
7. Unlike the sleepwalker or being in denial, when you are in SOS, you know you are lost.
8. In SOS you begin to question.
9. In SOS you have become intolerably desperate or weary as to the state of things in yourself and/or in your life.
10. SOS is a powerful catalyst for change, and it is a fragile time.

11. In SOS you desperately want to believe there is hope, light at the end of the dark tunnel.
12. SOS is deeply emotional and needs to be met with patience and kindness.
13. In SOS you finally reach outside for help, and that help needs to come from the outside. There is not enough clarity or presence of self to sustain or guide.
14. In SOS your beliefs are turned upside down.
15. In SOS your story of reality is shaken, and this can be very disorienting.
16. It takes courage to challenge our stories.
17. In SOS you begin to feel the craziness of negative thoughts and you begin to question their validity.
18. SOS renders you open.

THE LIVING PRACTICE #7
Exploring SOS

Creating, Experiencing, Pause, Inquiry, and Transformation

Exploring the SOS Phase in Your Life

Find a quiet place for contemplation while considering the following:

1. Are you in the SOS Phase? If yes, write about what is going for you and your life that has brought you to this point. What is the crisis, the trauma, the experiences, the beliefs that underscore this time in your life?

2. What do you need? For example, when I was in the SOS Phase I needed people to stop judging me. I needed to feel safe, I needed someone to listen to me. I needed someone to understand what I was going through and who could assure me that I would be okay. *Let yourself really open to everything you need.* Make a list. Write everything down. Don't hold back. Remember, the dam has burst and it is important to let your needs be heard by you.

3. What is your emotional state? How and where do you experience these emotions in your body? Again, don't hold back. Suppressing or denying your feelings is part of what created the SOS Phase.

4. What longings have you been suppressing or denying? Again, don't hold back. Denying what is important to you and how you truly want to live is part of what has brought you to this crisis point. Remember, your life path is uniquely yours, and you have a right to follow your soul's yearnings.

5. Is there someone in your life you feel safe with, who will listen and love you just the way you are? Write down his or her name. If there is more than one, write down each their names. If no one comes to mind, spend some time considering that perhaps there is someone from your past, a teacher or a relative whom you felt a connection with, and write down their name(s). Animals are wonderful at giving unconditional love. Do you have or have you had any animals that love or have loved you? If yes, write down their names. Consider your relationship to Spirit, God, the Divine. Write down the names of saints, angels, deities, the God of your understanding. Look at the names you have written. Look at them often, so that in this deeply felt and changing place

of SOS, you can see that you are not alone, that even now you are loved.

6. Once you have made a list of names, I want you to write down a day and time when you will reach out to at least one of them, to ask them if they will sit with you and listen as you read to them everything you wrote down in questions 1–4. Tell them that you are not seeking advice, just a loving heart to listen and receive you just as you are.

7. If you are not in the SOS Phase right now, have you ever been? If yes, write about what was happening in you and your life at that time.

Inward Journey to Feel Safe, Supported, and Loved

Find a comfortable place to sit or lie down. Close your eyes and focus on your breathing, noticing the state of your breathing… You might discover that your breath is shallow or fast or anxious or deep and quiet. After discovering the quality of your breathing, take three long, slow, deep breaths with the intention to open and relax your body and your mind… If you are already relaxed, this will support you dropping even deeper into an opened state of awareness.

See yourself walking through a brightly flowered meadow toward a wood in the distance. It is sunny and warm. You watch a butterfly move quickly from one flower to another, and then it comes to rest on the back of your hand. You stop walking and look with wonder at this fragile, multicolored being who has chosen this moment to be with you.... You smile.... In the next moment it lifts off, and you begin walking again.

The forest is now right in front of you. You leave the meadow and enter a path in the cool, shaded wood. You get lost in thought as you walk, not paying attention to the path or to where you are going.... Suddenly you realize you have lost the path and you don't know where you are. You look around for direction. You begin to feel frightened, lost, and alone. You remember that this feels a little like the panic you feel when you are unsure, in crisis, calling for help. You keep walking and you start to call out for help... Day is fading and the sunlight that had previously drifted through the treetops diminishes. The forest is quiet and dark. You stop walking.... You stand very still, listening. Again, you call for help. You feel a sense of the old panic returning.

Just then, the moon shines bright through the forest. The path you had previously believed was lost is now clearly lit by moonlight. The panic you had begun to feel is subsiding.... You notice that standing on the path in front of you is a beautiful Angel. The Angel has broad wings and is smiling at you with love. It stretches its arms toward you and you run to the Angel... It wraps its arms and wings around you. Your breathing grows deep and quiet, just like the forest. Your body relaxes in the Angel's arms. You feel safe now and loved... The Angel lifts you up and carries you back to the meadow. Once there, the Angel gently puts you down. You look at the Angel with gratitude.

The Angel wants to give you a gift so that whenever you are in crisis, calling for help, in a state of SOS, you can use it as a reminder that you are never alone. Divine help is always close by. Take a few moments to receive the Angel's gift.... This gift is uniquely created for you. Trust whatever you see, feel or hear. After you receive your gift, the Angel, just like the butterfly, lifts off and fades into the beautiful moonlit sky above you. You stand there in the meadow, warm and secure, knowing you are always guided and you are always loved....

Gently bringing this journey to a close, focus again on your breath. Slowly open your eyes and when you are ready, sit up. Spend some time writing about your experience of the journey. In particular, you may want to write or draw an image of the gift you received from your Angel.

Gently take in your surroundings before you stand up and go about the rest of your day.

An Affirmation to Help You in the SOS Phase

"I am divinely guided. No matter how difficult the circumstances, Spirit is always with me, helping me to remember that I am safe, loved, and never alone. I am being healed."

8

PHASE 4: KNOWLEDGE AND RESOURCES

*"Knowing others is intelligence,
Knowing yourself is true wisdom."*

—TAO TE CHING,
translated by Stephen Mitchell

The Knowledge and Resources Phase of remembering the truth of who you are is a renaissance for the spirit. It follows that the chaos experienced during SOS would send us running, thirsting for understanding. Knowledge and resources offers us that understanding and helps to guide us back on to the path of wholeness. When we have reached this phase, we are ready to be honest, to name what isn't working and to begin the active search for answers. In this chapter, we will explore how acquiring knowledge and resources works directly to heal the Five Obstacles that impede the awareness of the truth within us.

1. THE TRAUMA AND THE WOUND

Another client had also lost his way. He was an African-American man named Stephen, and like Marco, successful, at the top of his game. One day, Stephen realized that his life just didn't make sense anymore. He had strayed so far from the dreams of his youth. Driven in his work, much to the exclusion of anything or anyone else, he got wound tighter and tighter. Joy, passion, adventure, and fun had become things of the past. Now it was just work, work, work.

When Stephen started coming to me for sessions, he shared with me how important his spiritual connection had been to him as a young man. He shared that in his youth he read many books on Christ's teachings and Eastern Philosophy and how he found solace in those pages where it was written that we are love and light. He went on to say, "As I became immersed in my work and in raising a family, that spiritual connection faded and almost felt ridiculous." I assured Stephen that I understood. At one time, I also had strayed from the deep knowledge that I was made of light and that *all creation was infused with this same beauty.*

(Pause for a moment to consider:
Bring your awareness into the center of your heart.
You are part of all that is, all creation,
infused with divine light. Sensing into your heart
right now... feel this light inside...it lives in you.)

Now desperate and his soul starved for recognition, Stephen's very sense of what the world calls "sanity" was on edge. When he came to me, he was in SOS, calling out for help. I suggested that it might be the conditioning of the world around him trying to quell his deep knowledge of the truth that was insane, not him. I went on to tell him that it was the sanity in his soul that had spoken to him by saying, "Something is off here, and I will help you find your way to your real self."

I remember one day when he showed up at my door for his fourth session. The man who had always arrived impeccably dressed now had ice cream stains on his shirt, and his hair was disheveled. He looked frightened. He told me he had gotten lost coming to my office. I heard that not only literally but also desperately as, "I'm lost, and I need help." So, in the beginning of our work, I kept assuring him that he would be okay, that he would find his way back to his true self, and that I was here to support him. This is the level of work you establish in the SOS Phase.

> "You necessarily have to be lost,
> before you're found."
> —T. Scott McLeod,
> *The Light in the Darkness*

As our work continued, we moved into the Knowledge and Resource Phase by exploring the origin and consequences of Stephen's early childhood trauma and wound. He shared that he was wanted and loved as a child. However, he had been born with a physical inability to absorb nutrition. The result was that in his first several months of life, he was essentially starving. He would cry for hours on end, much to the distress of his parents. His parents kept seeking medical help until they were finally able to resolve the issue. By then, the wound of abandonment, helplessness, and not having enough had left its mark on Stephen. His reaction to his wound set him on a course of making sure he had enough. And so, he worked very hard to make sure he had enough money, enough possessions, and enough control so that he would never "starve" again.

An important aspect about the wound is that the soul has come to heal the misconceptions connected to it. These misunderstandings arise out of the child's interpretation of the trauma/wound. In other words, while the experience of the trauma and the wound are painful and unfortunate, secondary woundings—messagess, beliefs, and defenses, are created out of our misunderstandings. This results in secondary pain. It is a hard pain, whereas the primary pain, that of the original trauma/wound, is a soft pain that yields to healing when released.

There is no getting around early childhood experiences that are painful. They are part of life, and all humans experience them. However, as humans in our capacity for self-awareness, we tend to take those experiences as an indication that something is wrong with us, *because* we had the painful experiences. Conversely, we believe that if we are "good" we would not experience a trauma, nor would we have an emotional wound. Some go even further to believe that they would never have a physical illness if they were "good."

Therefore, in the Knowledge and Resources Phase of our work together, I taught Stephen about the nature of the trauma and the wound; that they are unavoidable and that they play an integral role in what his soul came to heal. Stephen is a brilliant man. And while he could conceptualize what I was saying, his emotions were still very shaky. This led him to explore the negative messages he had received.

2. THE NEGATIVE MESSAGES YOU RECEIVED

Parental Messages

Though his parents loved him, Stephen felt his parent's helplessness in their not being able to alleviate his discomfort in those first months of his life and their fear that they might lose him. It is important to note that *messages do not have to be communicated directly from the parents or society* toward the child. Each child enters this world like a sponge. They are undifferentiated from their parents and their environment, so they absorb all the energies, feelings, and events around them as if all were part of the child. This absorption often strengthens the misconceptions the soul has come to heal. For Stephen, some of the parental messages he received were not intentionally directed at him. But his parent's helplessness became his own, and his inability to absorb food and milk meant that something was defective in him.

Societal Messages

As Stephen grew up, the societal message he received was that he needed to cover his feelings of helplessness by being strong. The message he received is, "Men have to be strong." To have feelings like helplessness or sadness would indicate inherent weakness, and that, for a man, is often socially unacceptable. This message of strength was often expressed through him as being as physically strong and emotionally tough as possible. Stephen spoke about his popularity in high school and how he would often ridicule the "weaker" boys to cover his own fear of helplessness.

Self-Generated Messages

Stephen's mantra became, "I'm tough." That is the message he told himself over and over. In doing so, he began to cover the deep, compassionate feelings he had felt as a child. He had loved animals as a young boy—his dog had been his best friend. But as he got older, that softness did not fit the message of "I'm tough," and he moved away from his natural love for animals.

In the Knowledge and Resources Phase of our work, I knew that re-education was an important element for Stephen to be willing to open again. I introduced him to different authors, people who were well recognized in the field of self-transformation. I introduced him to musical CDs and audio files that helped him replace his negative messages with positive ones, and I introduced him to mindfulness movement and meditation. Remember that while the SOS Phase is desperate, the Knowledge and Resources Phase is akin to a person dying of thirst. They voraciously seek the knowledge that will quench their pain and calm their spirit. I remember the day when Stephen came into my office with a smile on his face. He had been listening to a song, "I Love Myself the Way I Am," written by Jai Josef's on *Loving Your Self: Songs & Meditations*: Louise Hay and Jai Josefs. I could see that the Knowledge and Resource Phase had reached what I call *the saturation point* in him. Saturation is when the positive messages, the new, are finally seeping in. This gives us reprieve from the feelings of being lost in the dark and helpless. Positive saturation brings the direct experience of peace and light.

> *"As a single footstep will not make*
> *a path on the earth,*
> *so a single thought will not make*
> *a pathway in the mind.*
> *To make a deep physical path,*
> *we walk again and again.*
> *To make a deep mental path,*
> *we must think over and*
> *over the kind of thoughts we wish*
> *to dominate our lives."*
> —Henry David Thoreau

On my own journey, I moved out of the SOS Phase in the

early 1980s and into the Knowledge and Resources Phase. My ignorance and pain had had enough, and I was ready to open to something new. I found a little book titled *Where Are You Going*, by Swami Muktananda, an Indian Saint. Reading it was the first time I felt permission to deeply consider the question, "Where was I going?" For several years, I had just been going with the program of illness, pain, and depression. I had not considered that perhaps I had a say in the matter and that I could do something about it.

I read that book from cover to cover, absorbing the truth in each word. I drank it in. Swami Muktananda wrote of the soul's journey and how it was important to tend to the soul and its longing during your life. I knew in my heart this what I needed. And like Stephen, for the first time in several years I, too, had felt a smile on my face. Reading that book gave me so much hope that I went on to share it with several people along the way.

NEGATIVE BELIEFS

Stephen had formed many negative beliefs out of the experience of his wound and negative messages. One belief was "life is hard." Another was "there is not enough for everyone." A third belief was that he had to be calculating to make sure he got more than his share, so that figuratively he wouldn't starve to death. These beliefs caused Stephen to grow cynical. He became self-absorbed. His humor was often sarcastic, meant to cut others down so that he could feel superior. But as I wrote earlier, *negative beliefs are not part of the truth of who we are. They are the distorted beliefs of who we think we are.* Deep in Stephen's very wise soul, he knew this. That is why the day came when he was no longer able to believe the lies he had lived for so long. For folks like Stephen, who had such a strong spiritual connection as a child, the fall from that connection can be particularly painful. Unlike others who might keep "one toe" connected to their spiritual pursuits, Stephen had literally cut that part of himself off in his effort to "be strong." That is why he felt so utterly lost when his cynicism no longer worked for him.

The Knowledge and Resources Phase is the pursuit of understanding. Just as many others and I have done, Stephen spent large amounts of time in the library and bookstores, gathering books on subjects that spoke truth to him. He began attending lectures, workshops, and ongoing spiritual groups. He discovered a nondenominational church where fellowship was important and where religious dogma was minimum. He explored Qigong, Continuum, Yoga and Tai

Chi, to connect his burgeoning awareness with his physical body. As he grew in his understanding, he was ready to deal with the once impenetrable defense system he had constructed to protect himself.

3. DEFENSE SYSTEMS AND JUDGING

As stated earlier in the book, our defense systems are an automatic reaction to anything or anyone that threatens our sense of safety and our sense of self, whether real or imagined. In the Knowledge and Resources Phase, *you have entered the early stage of self-awareness* and therefore you begin to notice when you are in defense. Knowledge is *educating the self to orient to the truth* rather than the false. What is false is the projection of our fears and beliefs onto the world. Orienting oneself to the truth requires taking up the practice of self-inquiry.

For Stephen, this was a huge portal for him to go through. He had grown so accustomed to defending against everything and everyone that it was challenging even to pause and ask, "Am I really being threatened here, are my safety and physical person at risk?" As Stephen began to ask himself these questions, he usually found the answer to be "no." He realized he was just reacting to an uncomfortable feeling or situation. In place of the automatic defense, a sense of security and "enoughness" began to arise that until this point, had eluded him. His ability to be clear about when his defense was necessary and when it wasn't, was still shaky. But he was glimpsing the truth, and these glimpses alleviated his suffering. This motivated him to keep growing.

(Pause for a moment to consider:
Have you been in defense today?
If yes, was it necessary, or was it a habitual reaction?
If it was necessary, why?)

I remember in the Knowledge and Resources Phase when I became aware of my defense system. My defense was simply to withdraw my awareness out of my body. So, while I was physically present, the rest of me escaped. In other words, *I* wasn't present. After my divorce, I felt insecure and shy around men. I had never been like that before. I loved men and, in fact, most of my friends were men. However, the violence in my marriage had left me scarred and scared. My brother and sister-in-law would arrange dinner parties and invite eligible men over to meet me. My family and students know as me as open, always ready for a good laugh, gregarious. However, at that time, if you put me at a dinner table with a guy who might find me interesting, I would close like a clam and emotionally and intellectually disappear. I could barely contribute to a conversation. After the poor fellow would leave, my brother would ask what was the matter with me? He said my I.Q. dropped about 100 points at the dinner table. We laughed at this observation, but inside of myself I was afraid that I might make the mistake of being with a man who was violent again. This fear prompted the automatic defense of withdrawing (freeze and flight)in me.

I also became aware of how much I judged others without even knowing them. My fear that any guy who walked through the door was someone to be afraid of was judging. Remember, *judging closes the door to curiosity and understanding.* My judging prevented me from getting to genuinely know the person. And at this point I kept the door to understanding myself closed by judging myself as defective when it came to my relationships with men. Again, the good news is that I had started the awkward process of awakening. So, while I was powerless not to defend at that time, I *knew* when I was defending. I kept reading books and saying positive affirmations, acquiring the necessary tools to support myself in shifting from a defended life to an undefended one.

4. BELIEVING YOUR STORY IS ALL THERE IS

It takes a lot to wake up to the realization that you are more than your story and that there is a lot more to "reality" than what your story would have you believe.

In the Knowledge and Resources Phase, the seeker can create opportunities to be exposed to many ways of thinking, different paths, and different philosophies. What I have noticed over my years of seeking the truth of who we are is that no matter where you look, the unified truth, the truth that love is all there ever was or is, can be found everywhere. I find that infinitely comforting. I have studied with many teachers from many different disciplines over the years. And while their language of the work and approach varied, at their core, *the same truth was always present*. As Mahatma Gandhi said, "Truth is one, paths are many."

During this phase, Stephen began to look at the story of his life differently. While he still tended to cling to "my story is the only reality," a new awareness was growing in him. And this awareness would say, *"Maybe* I am not restricted by the painful experiences of my story. *Maybe these experiences are here to teach me.*" It is important to note the word, *maybe*. In the Knowledge and Resources Phase, we are still trapped in our story, and yet, doubt about the story and hope that maybe there is something more has begun to shine through. *See how far you have come from sleepwalking* (non-questioning the experiences of your life) to knowledge and resources (maybe there is more here than meets the eye)!

During the Knowledge and Resources Phase I was prompted to leave the part of the world where I had locked myself into an identity and story that, "I was the sick and depressed one." At my soul's urging, I felt compelled to embark on what the eminent twentieth-century philosopher Joseph Campbell referred to in his book *The Hero with a Thousand Faces* as the Hero's Journey.

The Hero/Heroine's Journey is a great way to challenge your limiting story. It encompasses twelve stages in three distinct worlds. Below is a summary of the three worlds.

Departure

The first world is the ordinary world where the hero/heroine lives. This is the world they know and that knows them. This is the world of fixed identity and patterns. S/he must leave their tribe and their world (this can be metaphoric or literal) and *venture into the unknown*. Just as the great explorers throughout history have done, the hero/heroine must leave everything they know behind (again, this can be done by suspending belief in your story or, as in my case, physically removing myself from all known surroundings that were holding my story in place). The hero/heroine must answer the inner call of adventure. The risk is to enter the unknown, where change and transformation is inevitable.

I remember beginning my own heroine's journey (which is part of the Awakening journey). I was excited and terrified. I was afraid of letting go what I had come to define as *me*. Over the years, I had insulated myself with layers of judgement, defenses, negative stories and beliefs about myself. Now, outside of my conditioned, ordinary world I was entering the unknown. By doing so, the insulated layers or 'cobwebs' as I call them, were destined to clear.

Initiation

The second world is the special world. It is the world of challenges, tests, and ordeals. *The hero/heroine must enter the 'dark forest'* (descend into the psyche's unconscious) to search out, find, confront and resolve the inner conflicts (the unpleasant emotions beneath the stories, thoughts, defenses, negative messages and beliefs that are limiting the individual).

There is no clear forward path in the 'dark forest'. This is the initiation. Because no clear path exists it is disorienting, and that can be terrifying. The path must be made by the self, guided by Spirit. It is made *with each courageous step taken* into the unconscious mind (the place where one has spent a lifetime burying the pain, anxiety and fears that are deemed unacceptable). By delving into the unconscious, it becomes conscious. In mythology, it is akin to the hero entering the dark forest to find and slay the dragon or seize the sword. By confronting and resolving the conflict, the hero/heroine is awarded the treasure.

For me, as the 'cobwebs' began to fall away, my fear and sense of having lost my bearings increased. There was no path for me to follow. Without the familiar stuck places, I was left to delve into my unconscious and confront the raw dragons that I had suppressed. These dragons were my intense thoughts and feelings of self-hatred, fear of myself and the pain of my wound, which had formed out of my original misunderstanding of the trauma and wound I had experienced. Somehow or another, I was led step-by-step to the Judean desert in Israel. I now know that it was Spirit's infinite love for me that guided me there. Thus, my 'dark forest' was spent in the Judea, where Christ had spent forty days and nights in prayer and solitude. My time there however, was not a quiet one. As I walked and prayed, I was plunged into the depths of what had been, my unconscious despair. I began to feel the fears I had buried. I prayed for redemption. I prayed for healing. I prayed for reprieve from suffering. I prayed for acceptance and love. As I did this, beloved Spirit heard me and my self-hatred and misunderstandings were pulled to the surface of my awareness for me to conquer. As I courageously faced my deepest fears, their power over me began to dissolve.

Return

The third world is the return to the ordinary world. It is only after they have met and *resolved the ordeal that the hero/heroine is resurrected.* They have *received the gift of the liberated Self* by reclaiming the truth of who they are. They are now ready to jubilantly return home and be welcomed by their tribe. A new authentic Self has emerged, and the false self has been slayed, dissolved, and healed. Such was much of my journey in the Knowledge and the Resources Phase. I left everyone and everything I knew behind. I spent fifteen months traveling the world, and finally, with courage, I met the dragons within me. While a big part of me was still waiting to go more deeply into the feeling work in the Opening Phase, I had begun to challenge my story. In return I received a new experience of myself and a sense of freedom blossomed.

Taking the Hero/Heroine Journey can help us to rediscover our inner resources as well. For me, I rediscovered my sense of humor and light-heartedness. I have found the adventure of being human to be an endless source for good-spirited humor. It is a humor that unifies us as one human family. I have often told my students that if I couldn't laugh, I would have been gone a long time ago. On Stephen's journey, he rediscovered his love of music. He has become a beautiful pianist. Playing and composing music has helped him to explore and express his spiritual nature.

Another important aspect of how to utilize your story in the Knowledge and Resources Phase is by *understanding that your story holds clues to what kind of knowledge would be useful for you*. For example, part of my story was being married to an alcoholic. In my Knowledge and Resources Phase, I read several books about alcoholism and then I read about codependency to help me see my role with alcoholism. I found my way to Al-Anon. This led me to search deeper into my own family history with alcoholism and addiction. Our stories will point the way for the knowledge and resources we need, in order to heal and return to the truth of who we are.

The Knowledge and Resources Phase will support you in realizing that your story and each of your life experiences serve a purpose. You are not a victim of situation and circumstance. This burgeoning awareness can help you understand, that you have the power *in you* to discover the purpose of your life experiences and to open to the lessons and gifts they offer. Ultimately, on the journey we learn that our stories, while useful, are just stories, and they cannot define who we are.

5. BELIEVING YOUR THOUGHTS

One of the most significant things we can learn in the Knowledge and Resources Phase is the power our thoughts have over us. Stephen spent many sessions investigating why he had adamantly believed his negative thoughts for so many years. Like Stephen in this phase, I too had been shocked to discover how my negative thinking was essentially killing me. The distorted thoughts that arise in the mind are based on a person's perception and interpretation of their story and subsequent worldview.

While typically still held in bondage by the mind, the self is beginning to doubt and question the accuracy of the mind's thought process. I have a client who recently shared that he just couldn't stand to be around people he found annoying. He adamantly believed his thoughts that certain people are annoying and as such you just need to stay away from them. Spirit, in its infinite wisdom, kept putting those same people right in front of him. He finally decided to question *his thoughts* about annoying people. He shared with me that his questioning had opened his mind. He began to see how his thoughts limited his ability to connect with others. When he stopped believing the thought "that certain people are annoying," he could experience the uniqueness of each person beneath the behavior that his thinking had convinced him was irritating.

We may even begin to question the whole process of thought by asking, "Are any of my thoughts real? Am I making this whole thing up?" These are healthy questions because, they mean the self has truly embarked on the hero/heroine's journey into the unknown. Unknown territory opens us to new experiences, discoveries and exciting, unlimited possibilities.

Once you have done the legwork in the Knowledge and Resources Phase—sought out mentors, groups, books and other educational tools, and your own inner resources—you are prepared to go into deeper work. That work begins in the Opening Phase. This phase involves going into the "belly of the beast" and experiencing the pain you have locked away and spent your life avoiding.

CHAPTER #8

The Key Points to Knowledge and Resources

1. The Knowledge and Resources phase is the active pursuit of ongoing support and understanding.
2. You are capable of being honest with yourself and can name what isn't working in your life.
3. You realize that you need help to support your healing.
4. This is an early stage of self-awareness.
5. You begin to understand the obstacles in your life and their impact.
6. In this phase, you begin to acquire the tools to deal with the obstacles.
7. The seeker can create opportunities to be exposed to many different paths and philosophies.
8. Knowledge educates the self to orient to the truth within them rather than false projections, fears, and beliefs.
9. Saturating the mind with the positive helps to replace the negative tapes.
10. The accumulation of knowledge reaches a saturation point where the self is beginning to experience a sense of wholeness within.

11. We begin to understand that our story holds clues to what kind of knowledge would be useful in healing the obstacles.
12. We consider that there may be more to life than our story would have us believe.
13. We begin to question the validity of our thoughts.

THE LIVING PRACTICE #8
Discovering Knowledge and Resources

Creating, Experiencing, Pause, Inquiry, and Transformation

Find a quiet place for contemplation to consider and write about the following:

1. What isn't working in your relationship to yourself or your life? Where are you unhappy or dissatisfied? What is the issue? How long has this been going on? Do you have any idea as to the origin of it?

2. What don't you understand about the issue(s) that trouble you? What do you want to understand? For example, when I realized my husband was an alcoholic, I did not understand why this was happening in my life and I desperately wanted to understand my part in it.

3. Once you have identified the issue regarding what isn't working in you or your life, spend some time

searching the Internet for books and/or CDs about the issue. Make a list of all the ones you are drawn to reading or listening.

4. Once you have your list, order at least one of the books/CDs or go to your local library to see if they have the book/CD you want or similar ones about the issue.

5. Next, spend some more time searching the Internet for therapists (there are many benefical therapeutic modalities), groups, and/or workshops that you think might be supportive in your quest for healing. Write down the ones that appeal to you. Make a commitment to contact at least one of the names on the list.

6. Make a list of questions that are important for you to ask when you contact the person/group/workshop you have chosen. For example, you may want to ask them about their level of experience, their fees (if it's not a free service), how often they meet if it's a group, and so on.

7. Explore different types of mindfulness movements to support your physical health, emotional well-being and burgeoning awareness. (Even if you are physically restricted, most mindfulness movements can be adapted).

8. Spend time going inside of yourself to discover some of your own inner resources. Write down the ones that spontaneously come to you, even if your judgmental self tries to negate them.

Inward Journey to Open to Knowledge and Resources
Find a comfortable place to sit or lie down. Close your eyes and focus on your breathing, noticing the state of your breathing... You might discover that your breath is shallow or fast or anxious or deep or quiet. After discovering the quality of your breathing, take three long, slow, deep breaths with the intention to open and relax your body and your mind... If you are already relaxed, this will support you dropping even deeper into an opened state of awareness.

See yourself standing outside a very large stone building with wide steps that lead to its entrance. Over the door is a sign that reads "House of Knowledge and Resources." You feel hope as you look at the sign. You climb the steps and go to the door. It opens automatically... You step inside... You find yourself in a large, circular room with marble floors, large windows and a gilded ceiling. The room is flooded with light. The circular wall of the room has five doors that lead to interior rooms. Each door is marked with a blank sign. The rooms and signs have been waiting for you to determine what kind of knowledge and resources you need to find and explore in your life... These signs will be designated *especially for you.*

You see a beautiful chair in the center of the room with a small table in front of it. On the table is a sheet of paper and a silver pen... Next to the pen is a large glass of crystal-clear water for you to drink if you are thirsty. You sit down in the chair and pick up the pen... You look at the first door to determine what knowledge and resources you would like this room to hold for you... Once you decide, you write it down on the sheet of paper. You look up, and quite magically, the sign on the first door has been etched with the words you have just written.

Happy with your creation, you go on to study each of the other four blank signs. Your contemplation helps you decide what type of knowledge and resource you would like each room to contain, in support of your journey home to the truth of who you are.... For example, you might consider a room with a sign that reads, "The Archives of Learning to Love Yourself." Take time to discover each specific sign... Each time you decide on one and write it down, the sign above the door becomes etched with the words you have chosen. When all five signs have been written, you relax back into the comfort of the chair... You feel empowered, having decided for yourself what kinds of knowledge and resources you need. You take a sip of the cool water... It is so refreshing.

The chair begins to slowly move in a clockwise circular motion so that you can study each of your designated signs... You feel satisfied with having chosen so wisely, the areas of interest you wish to learn about. These areas or subjects will support you in gaining insight and wisdom. They will help you remember the truth of who you are... Eventually, your eyes come to rest on one door and its accompanying sign... You feel this door calling to you in *this moment*. It's as if it is saying, 'begin here.' The chair stops moving in front of your chosen door... You smile as you get up and walk toward it, confident and excited about what awaits you inside. You turn the doorknob and the door opens. You feel supported, completely aware that the knowledge and resources you need are here to help guide you back into your inherent wholeness...

Gently bringing this inward journey to a close, focus again on your breath... Slowly open your eyes, and when you are ready, sit up. Spend some time writing about your experience of the journey. In particular, you may want to write about the five signs of knowledge and resources that you have chosen for yourself and the one that calls to you now.

Gently take in your surroundings before you stand up and go about the rest of your day.

**Affirmation to Help You During
the Knowledge and Resources Phase**

"As I reach out for understanding and support I am led to the perfect individuals, groups, books and classes/workshops that will help me to remember the truth of who I am."

9

Phase 5: Opening

"And now here is my secret,

a very simple secret:

It is only with the heart

that one can see rightly;

what is essential is invisible

to the eye."

—ANTOINE DE SAINT-EXUPÉRY,
The Little Prince

Throughout time, mystics (those who seek spiritual truths that elude the rational mind) speak of both the agony and ecstasy intrinsic in the search. Caroline Myss, in her book *Anatomy of the Spirit,* writes, "Although the spiritual path ... can be arduous, no matter how much physical misery these mystics encountered along the way, none of them ever asked to return to ordinary consciousness." In the Opening Phase, we have achieved this level of understanding—there is no going back to sleep.

The Opening Phase offers us an opportunity to *go into the pain of our emotional wounds and release the anger and sorrow held captive there.* This pain, as we know from previous phases, has never been absent. It has just been buried and often expressed in destructive and unconscious ways. Now, we have the opportunity to make that pain conscious. It is by going through our agony that we are lifted into the ecstatic experiences of connectedness, belonging, and peace.

An unfortunate message that most people receive is that some feelings are acceptable and others are not. It is okay to be joyful; it is not okay to be sad. It is okay to feel hope;

it is not okay to feel despair. It is okay to feel love; it is not okay to feel anger. With all the "should" and "should-nots" running around, it is no surprise there is so much road rage. Feelings, both "positive" and "negative," are part of being human. It is inhuman to expect otherwise. And yet this is what we often do. Early on, children are usually taught to quell their natural emotions and conform to the conditioned adult world around them. This often leads the growing child to feelings of shame and to *masking their feelings and their authentic self*. The result can be numbing, a deadening, as people are left feeling a loss. This is true because we have given up part of our naturalness in order to conform.

Also true is that because our feelings are deeply buried, we cannot even connect with the origin of the loss. If we refuse the "negative," or what some refer to as the "inconvenient" or unacceptable emotions within us, you can be sure that the "positive" ones are muted or made artificial at times. So, the eruption that occurs in SOS is good. For it is in that phase the authentic self is shouting, "I am sick and tired of walking around half-dead, and I am not going to take it anymore." This eruption, while necessary for healing, needs to be guided in safe and skilled environments that can support the emotional expression and release needed for healing. Fundamentally, *the safe expression and release of buried emotional pain* is what the Opening Phase is all about.

> *"Each time we drop our masks and meet heart-to-heart...*
> *Each time we are able to remain open to suffering,*
> *despite our fear and defensiveness, we sense a love in us*
> *which becomes increasingly unconditional...*
> *Awakening from our sense of separateness is what*
> *we are called to do in all things."*
> —Ram Dass

1. THE TRAUMA AND THE WOUND

Karma blew into my practice as seemingly free-spirited as her name. A young, hip, white artist with arms and shoulders tattooed in colorful ink, she sat down and began chatting away. Articulate and bright, she talked of a troubled past with drugs, multiple transfers of schools as a child, and sexual abuse as if she were talking about the weather. I listened, intrigued by this young woman. When she spoke, she lit up a little too much, and her words came just a little too fast. Her rapid speech seemed a ruse to cover her pain.

During the first few sessions, we explored her past, particularly, her childhood. Her mother loved her but had been undependable. Her biological father left soon after she was born, and her stepfather hated her. He would ridicule her, shame her, and tell her she was worthless while treating his biological children kindly. When she turned nine, her stepfather started making nightly visits to her bedroom. Karma left home when she was thirteen and went to live with an older man. He was violent and repeatedly beat her. One time, his fist landed her in the hospital. At that point, she left him and started making a living on the streets as a prostitute. Super bright and restless, she applied to a local college and was accepted. That was a turning point for Karma. She stopped using drugs, got off the streets, and concentrated on her studies. Now, five years later with a diploma in hand, she felt ready to "do the work."

During her fourth session, I spoke with her about her rage, though she had covered it up beautifully with her fast-paced monologues. She looked at me and nodded silently. I asked her if she felt ready to do some work with her anger. Karma said, "Yes." "Good," I said. And then I went on to tell her that we would begin the anger work in her next session. I wanted to give her time to feel into it and to let her know that she was in control and had a voice in the decision.

The sense of personal choice and empowerment is key in the Opening phase. This point is so important that I need to explain it further. When we block our so-called "negative" emotions, they begin to take on power. So much so that people are often afraid to feel them out of fear that they will lose control and hurt themselves or someone else in the process. Therefore, *it is vital that the person doing this level of work be in a safe, supportive environment* while understanding that *they are in charge of how deep they want to go.*

During Karma's next session, we explored her feelings toward her stepfather. In the previous sessions, she had spoken calmly about him. Now, going deeper, Karma shared that what hurt most was that her stepfather did not call her by her name. Instead, he called her "Dog." For her, his dehumanization of her by calling her Dog underscored the sexual abuse she had experienced and left her feeling totally worthless.

At this point I introduced a therapeutic tool called the Bataka. A Bataka is shaped like a very soft baseball bat. It can be used therapeutically to hit pillows. Essentially, the act of hitting increases the energy in a person, and this puts pressure on the defenses we use to stop ourselves from feeling. The increase in energy can break through our defenses so that we are free to feel the rage and grief we have suppressed.

It is important to note that *there are many ways to access suppressed feelings*. Doing the work of *accessing, expressing, releasing, and integrating* one's feelings needs to be done in a way that supports the individual doing the work. For some people, hitting a pillow may not be the right choice. Therefore, it is good to work with a skilled therapist who can help you go into your anger and grief in a way and at a pace that is healthy for you.

I asked Karma if she would like to use the Bataka as a tool to help her go deeper into her feelings. She said yes. I then asked her what she would like to say to her stepfather. I suggested she find one short statement to focus on while hitting. She said, "I want to call him 'Monster'." "Okay", I said, "that's good." Karma began hitting the pillows. At first, her hits were tentative and slow. I encouraged her to add the word "Monster" as she hit. Before she knew it, she was shouting out to her stepfather. She was hitting harder and faster, and her words became wrenching sobs from deep within her belly. After several minutes, she stopped hitting and fell into my arms. I held her and rocked her as she continued to cry. Through her tears she asked, "Why, why did he hurt me? It hurts so bad." I soothed her while assuring her that she was safe now, that she was good, and that she did not deserve to have been treated cruelly.

After her emotional flow subsided, which took quite a bit of time, we returned to our chairs to integrate her work before the session ended. She shared that she was utterly shocked by how hard she had hit and how hard she cried. She said she felt freer, lighter inside herself. As I looked at her face she looked tired, and at the same time soft and open.

I explained to her that what she had done was to go into her emotional wound and feel what is called the "original pain." We all have emotional wounds. *Trapped within the wound is the pain the child experienced at the time of the trauma.* That original pain is a felt experience. For a young child, totally dependent on others for survival, that *experience is felt like a matter of life or death*. The child, overwhelmed and unequipped to handle it, does what they need to do, in order to survive the experience: *They bury the pain*. This is what is called the "split." *The act of separating the self from the trauma and the painful feelings in the wound is "splitting."* All of us split to one degree or another from our "original pain." We cover it by creating secondary pain through our negative beliefs and defenses, stories, and thoughts.

2. THE NEGATIVE MESSAGES

Parental Messages

Karma received mixed messages about love. Her mother loved her but did not intercede when Karma's stepfather mistreated and abused her. This experience left Karma with a very mixed message about love from her mother. On the other hand, her stepfather's message about love was clear: "Love hurts; love is cruel." It was through these messages that Karma went on to choose men who hurt her in the name of love.

Societal Messages

Karma shared with me that she never felt safe during her childhood. She felt that since her stepfather got away with sexually molesting her and treating her badly, even in public, that perhaps the world did not care about her. From the lack of adult intervention either in school, church, or society in general, Karma got the message that children are not protected. As she grew older, Karma grew rebellious. She was also a deeply caring person. During her time on the streets she made it her mission to counter the negative societal messages by intervening when she saw underage girls being lured or trapped into prostitution.

Self-Generated Messages

For all her courage, and it took tremendous courage for Karma to lift herself out of the abusive path she had lived, she remained scarred by her own negative messages. Early on, her message to herself echoed her stepfather's. She told herself she was worthless and unlovable, and she proved it by choosing a lifestyle that was dangerous and destructive.

In the Opening Phase, we begin to work with the deep feelings and scars of the painful messages that constitute the secondary pain. For Karma, that meant feeling the wrenching heartbreak of having been repeatedly told by her stepfather and by herself that she was unlovable.

The messages we receive and generate are the foundation for our belief systems. Let's look at how Karma's messages formulated her negative beliefs.

Negative Beliefs

By the time she was thirteen, Karma had decided that the world was a cruel place and that there was no escaping this fact. She had formed this belief about life out of the years she lived with parental abuse and the messages that implied. Fortunately, Karma was resilient. In the Opening

Phase, she found the courage to challenge her belief. When Karma felt the pain of her wound and cried out, "Why did he hurt me?" she had finally given voice to the question that had lived in her since she was a child. In that moment, unbeknownst to her, she was challenging the message and belief that she was unlovable. What often arises in the child out of painful experiences is the belief that *they did something wrong* to have such experiences. So, for Karma, prior to the work she did in the Opening Phase, she had not dared to ask that question, because she had always believed that the answer would be that she was unlovable. Now, in asking the question and feeling her pain, she opened to the pure experience of loving, and through this she felt herself as lovable. *So much is healed when we let ourselves feel.*

I remember in my own Opening Phase. I was terrified to feel the rage inside me. I had punished myself for years for having such strong negative feelings. The message I had been telling myself was that I was bad to feel so much loss and hatred and that I had no right to be angry.

The first time that I publically opened and shared my feelings of hatred and rage, was at a workshop called "Growing through Grief." The facilitators were three compassionate individuals who had studied with Dr. Elisabeth Kubler-Ross, a Swiss M.D. fondly referred to as the "Queen of Death and Dying." Her landmark work opened the doors to the grieving process and shed light on the passages we encounter in the dying process.

The workshop I attended began on a Friday night. We began by sitting in a circle. There were about fifteen participants and the facilitators. In the middle of the circle was a big pile of telephone books and a rubber hose. The facilitators introduced the work by telling us that each of us would have the opportunity to work with our feelings by hitting the telephone books. They said that tonight, by way of introduction, each participant could practice by coming into the center of the circle, holding the hose, and hitting the telephone books a few times, just to get a feel for it. As I listened to them, I sat there in shock. I thought to myself, "This is crazy, evil, wrong. No good person would ever consider doing such a thing." And here I was. Truthfully, I had been afraid of my harsh feelings for years, because I thought I was evil for having them. And now I was being given the possibility of confronting them. Either I was going to find out that I really was bad or maybe, just maybe, I would experience something new. I trusted the person who recommended the workshop. She was one of my Al-Anon sponsors and one of the workshop facilitators. Her name was Bette, and she had already helped me so much. So, when my turn came to hold the rubber hose, I picked it up and studied it carefully. "Not so bad," I thought as I hit a few times and quickly put it down.

Over the next few days something extraordinary happened. When it came my time to "do the work," I got on my knees in front of the pile of telephone books, picked up the hose, and began hitting. Before I knew it, I was screaming at God for letting such terrible things happen to me in my life, and I was screaming at myself, "I hate me." Then my screaming turned to sobs. At some point, I looked up from the wrath and sorrow that had consumed me for years. Everyone in the circle was looking at me with love. They had not run out of the room when I screamed. They were not afraid of me. I had not hurt them with my rage. The only thing that lay waste in that room were the telephone books. They had been shredded to pieces, the pages scattered everywhere. I looked down at my hands and my fingers were bleeding. Bette came over and put her arms around me. "Badges of courage," she said as she gently placed Band-Aids on my bleeding fingers. At some point, I made my way to my feet and for the first time in years, I felt my feet on the ground. I felt that I belonged to humanity, and in belonging I felt an overwhelming love for myself, my parents, the folks in the room, and God.

This is the work of Opening.

3. THE DEFENSE SYSTEMS AND JUDGING

Prior to opening, our defense systems are pretty cemented into holding our emotions in check, or, expressing them in distorted ways. Following the illness in my 20s I had so many feelings of betrayal by God, my parents, and myself. However, I had a very strong defense system that would only allow me to feel anger toward myself. Whenever other feelings would try to surface, feelings that went way back to the wounds of my childhood, I would squelch them, judging myself by saying that I was wrong to have them. That was my defense. However, the work I did in the "Growing Through Grief" workshop was the catalyst that broke through my defenses so that I could finally feel and release the "negative" emotions inside of me.

The same was true for Karma and for the thousands of individuals I have had the privilege to support. With careful consideration of the timing to open, creating a safe and unconditionally loving space, and the loving invitation to feel, one is ready to penetrate the defenses, let go of judging, and release the storms inside. I believe that if we understood the importance and sacredness of this level of work, there would be less violence committed in the world.

4. BELIEVING YOUR STORY IS ALL THERE IS

Before I picked up the rubber hose and began hitting, I was convinced that all the negative messages embedded in my story were true. And yet, something inside me kept insisting that perhaps there was more to life than shame, pain, fear, anger, grief and disappointment. As a young child, I laughed. I was deeply loved. My parents had given my siblings and me freedom to create and play. Our imaginations, interests and opinions were encouraged. The natural world was our playroom. Overall, the days of my childhood were an invitation to fully engage with life. I had fun! At the same time, I felt sad when someone appeared lost or hurt, or when a being—be it a human being or animal—was being mistreated. On those occasions, even as a young child, I intervened.

I had also felt inexplicable feelings of "homesickness." I would often go outside in the evening and wistfully sing to the stars. I yearned for communion with God/Spirit/Source—*the all that is.*

As a teenager, though I had endured the torment of being bullied, I also had many experiences of joy and the adventure of being alive. I was deeply committed to causes that called for justice and healing. Like Karma, I had challenged the status quo. Because of my seeming fearlessness, I had earned the nickname "Mother Courage" from some of my friends. Most of them did not know that behind my genuinely sunny smile was a wall of pain from traumas and wounds I had endured along the way. Our lives are a blend of both positive and negative experiences. We all carry joy and heartbreak. In the Opening Phase, you finally release the dam of feelings, and this in turn frees you to feel the miraculous joy at the center of all life.

For Karma, that first session of releasing such deep feelings was, as I told her, the tip of the iceberg. We are not done with the pain from one round of release. Opening gave Karma a tool to be with her pain in a new way. It showed her that no matter what she is feeling, she is lovable and can tend to her pain in a loving, open way. It also opened the door to understanding her story, the events of her life, in a new way.

Whereas in the Knowledge and Resources Phase our stories give us clues, in the *Opening Phase our stories are the keys*. They are the keys to the doors our souls have come to walk through and heal so that, liberated, we can embrace the truth of who we are.

5. BELIEVING YOUR THOUGHTS

One of the miraculous events that happens in the Opening Phase is that *we finally bring the power of our thoughts together with the power of our feelings*. Prior to this they have, for the most part, been kept separate (the split). Only when we allow the two to be experienced together can we release, integrate, and heal the split. In Karma's case, she had been haunted by the memory and thought of being called "Dog" by the man who had systematically abused her. When she brought that thought together with her rage and grief and called him what she had been thinking but had been too terrified to feel, "Monster," she began to accept that what he had done to her was truly monstrous.

The beautiful result is that after such deep work, our thoughts begin to lose some of their power and their grip on us. Karma had been a prisoner to her thoughts about herself, her stepfather, and life. Now, through her courage to open, she had the ability to have a better perspective about her thoughts. This awareness promotes what I call the process of *spiritual maturation*. And when this happens, we are ready for the next phase, Committed.

Let's step through that door to discover the treasures that await anyone who commits to the daily work of walking the path of awakening.

CHAPTER #9

The Key Points to Opening

1. Opening is finding/creating safe environments for the expression and release of buried emotional pain.

2. A sense of personal choice and empowerment is essential in the Opening Phase.

3. In the Opening Phase, you decide when and how deeply you want to go into your feelings.

4. There are many healthy ways to access your suppressed feelings.

5. Opening is accessing, expressing, releasing, and integrating your "negative/inconvenient" feelings.

6. The act of separating the self and the event from the original pain of the wound is called "the split." Opening to the original pain helps to heal the split.

7. Feeling=Healing.

8. In the Opening Phase, our stories are the keys to the doors we have come to walk through and heal.

9. In opening we bring our thoughts and memories together with our emotions (healing the split).

10. Experiencing our thoughts and emotions together is the catalyst for releasing and integrating. This is part of the alchemical process of transformation.

11. When we release our buried feelings, our negative thinking begins to lose its power.

THE LIVING PRACTICE #9
Exploring Openings

Creating, Experiencing, Pause, Inquiry, and Transformation

Find a quiet place for contemplation to consider and write about the following:

1. What feelings and events have you been suppressing?

2. How long have you been burying your feelings?

3. How have you judged your "negative" feelings?

4. What are you fears about letting yourself feel your "inconvenient" or "negative" feelings?

5. Draw a picture of your "negative" feelings. After you have finished your drawing, take some time to feel what comes up for you as you look at it. Perhaps you may want to write about what you learned from your drawing.

6. After reading this chapter and the previous one, what resources do you have in place for yourself so that you can do the work of opening in a healthy way?

Inward Journey to Welcome Opening

Find a comfortable place to sit or lie down. Close your eyes and focus on your breathing, noticing the state of your breathing... You might discover that your breath is shallow or fast or anxious or deep or quiet. After discovering the quality of your breathing, take three long, slow, deep breaths with the intention to open and relax your body and your mind.... If you are already relaxed, this will support you dropping even deeper into an opened state of awareness.

Imagine that you are at home... You start to put some garbage in the trashcan and you notice that the can is filled and overflowing with garbage. You pull the heavy bag out and tie it securely. It is evening and the world is full of shadows, but you drag the bag outside to put it in a larger trash bin. As you go to lift the bag into the bin, you notice that the trash bin is also overflowing. You wonder, 'How did it get so full?' You peer inside the trash bin...

The top of the pile is covered with feelings and events from your life that were so painful you chose not to feel them. Instead, you buried them in the trash. You pull the top layer out and put it on the grass... You look back into the bin and find more buried painful experiences and feelings.... You pull them out...You continue to pull out layer after layer of buried feelings and experiences, spreading them all out onto the grass.... Finally, the bin is empty.

You look at your feelings of grief, sadness, anger, disappointment, fear, shame and the painful events connected to them scattered around the yard... As you look at them, you begin to realize they aren't so bad... You begin to feel compassion for all those buried feelings.... You wonder, "Why have I spent so much of my life burying these feelings?" From this vantage point, you can see back into your life, connecting events and thoughts with each of your buried feelings. Take some time for this... As you do this, you realize that all that these feelings have ever wanted was acceptance, recognition, love, and a safe place to be felt and released.... As you stand there looking at them, you make a commitment that you will not stuff these feelings back into the trash bin.... Instead, you commit to seeking out the right kind of support, either with a therapist or a group that provides a safe environment, so that you can do the work of opening, releasing, feeling, integrating, and healing... You notice that as you make this commitment, the feelings that looked so hard before, start to soften.

Gently bringing this inward journey to a close, focus again on your breath. Slowly open your eyes, and when you are ready, sit up. Spend some time writing about your experience of the journey. In particular, you may want to write about the feelings you buried, any events connected to them, and the commitment you have made to yourself to do the work of opening.

Gently take in your surroundings before you stand up and go about the rest of your day.

An Affirmation to Help You in the Opening Phase

"I understand that the way for me to feel free and happy is to do the work of safely releasing my buried, painful feelings. I trust that Spirit is watching over me with love as I open to my feelings."

10

PHASE 6: COMMITTED

"What lies behind us and what lies ahead of us are tiny matters compared to what lies within us."

—HENRY STANLEY HASKINS,
Meditations in Wall Street

When entering the Committed Phase, you have come to understand that *life itself* is the path to awakening. In this phase, all of life (inner and outer) is embraced as *the* living practice. Each day becomes an opportunity for you to participate in life as a conscious co-creator. As the Jesuit priest Pierre Teilhard de Chardin wrote, "We are collaborators in creation." Life is your classroom. Learn the principles of the Living Practice—create, experience, pause, inquire, transform, and then allow life to teach you. Each lived experience is an opportunity for inquiry and growth. Every experience you have is intended to serve your awakening. As you come to understand this, your ability to discern your intentions and consciously create will exponentially increase. This will lead you to a greater ability to move from reacting to responding in the moment. It is through this process that you become self-aware, and self-awareness is empowering.

> *"Life gives you exactly what you need to awaken."*
> —T. Scott McLeod

(Pause for a moment to consider:
Can you feel a sense of anticipation and freedom
as you consider meeting each day as new,
a wondrous opportunity to remember
the truth of who you are?)

Everyone is co-creating his or her life. Few are conscious of it. You've probably heard the saying, "Life happens." Or as someone said to me after recently celebrating the New Year, "I wonder what this year will bring?" When I heard that, I thought to myself, "I wonder what I will create and bring to this year?" The spontaneity of that thought in me revealed two things. The first is how my consciousness has genuinely shifted into being a conscious co-creator. You, too, will experience this natural shift in yourself in the Committed Phase. Secondly, I was gently reminded that many people really believe they have no say in their precious life. They often live feeling trapped, disempowered, and at the "mercy" of forces outside of themselves.

Self-awareness requires that you become completely responsible for your choices. Dr. Sigmund Freud wrote, "Most people do not really want freedom, because freedom involves responsibility, and most people are frightened of responsibility." Now, in your spiritual maturation, which is infinitely freeing, *there is no one left to blame*. With freedom comes responsibility. Understanding this is fundamental in the Committed Phase.

There is a popular concept called karma, which is often misunderstood. Many people think that karma is a negative. This is not true. Karma is a spiritual principle, meaning that each choice (intention and action) has a consequence, a result. Karma is cause/choice and effect/result. This is a liberating concept when you have accepted life as the classroom. *Results are no longer rewards or punishments; they are reflections*, aimed at helping you discern true from false, and in doing so, realize the shining truth of the Self.

It's also important to understand that while you may not or do not have the power to prevent certain situations or events such as an accident, illness, war, death, or the way others think of you, *you always have the power to consciously choose how to be in relationship with those events or situations*. The words "Bidden or Unbidden, God is present," written by Desiderius Erasmus, were inscribed over the doorway of Dr. Carl Jung's house. I have often reflected on the meaning of his words. In doing so, I have come to understand that God, Source, or whatever name you choose to attribute the Light of Pure Consciousness, is always present, even in sickness, war, and death. In the Committed Phase, you understand that your evolving place is not to lament about *why* things happen but rather to *discover ways to remain present and responsive with what is happening.*

Pierre Teilhard de Chardin wrote, "By virtue of Creation, and still more the Incarnation, nothing here below is profane for those who know how to see." In the Committed Phase, you are learning how to truly *see.*

Many of us on the path want to make little changes, hoping for big results. The razor's edge suggests that perhaps big changes are needed. Essentially, this calls for changing your perception of life and realizing that its fundamental purpose is an opportunity to learn, transform, and return to the truth of who you are.

"I'M READY FOR THE BIG CHANGE"

Joyce came me to energetic and sophisticated. She was in her early twenties and immersed in business as a mid-level manager. She walked into my office, immaculately dressed, with briefcase in hand. From all outward appearances, this woman was well put-together and had life on a string. I asked her why she had made an appointment. She looked directly at me and said, "I want more. I know there *must be more* to life than a career, a mortgage, marriage, and a family. I have always been interested in the big questions, such as why are we here, and who am I *really*?"

As I sat there listening to her, I could hear myself at the same age, thinking the same thoughts and asking the same questions. Now in my early sixties, I know the price for asking. I looked back at her and said, "If you are serious, I must tell you that the path of awakening to the truth of who you are is filled with pain and joy, uncertainty and revelation. It will teach you that the whole of your life is the spiritual journey." Her steady, direct gaze never wavered. "I understand," she replied, "and I'm ready."

I wasn't quite sure she really understood, and again I recalled myself at her age, certain that I knew what I was getting myself into by asking the "big" questions. "Well then," I said, "welcome to the mystical path of your life."

Over the next few years, Joyce traveled back and forth through the SOS, Knowledge and Resources, and Opening Phases. At times, she would become frustrated and just say, "Forget it, I don't care" and she would delve back into the material world as if that was all there is and all that mattered to her. After a few months, however, she would call and say, "I hate this, life just doesn't make sense, I am ready again." I understood. Many think that the path of awakening is a clear and conscious choice and that once you are on it, you stay committed to it. I know from my own experience that committing to the path usually comes after many periods of being with it and then leaving it. I discovered long ago that until you enter the Committed Phase, the path is a razor's edge.

When Joyce became truly ready to embrace *her whole life* as the living path to awakening, I knew that she had arrived in the Committed Phase. Once there, she became consistent in her search for the truth.

1. THE TRAUMA AND THE WOUND

By the time you have done enough work and settled into the commitment of living your life as the path, you have come down from the "pink cloud." The pink cloud is a popular twelve-step term. It describes the euphoric experience that accompanies early recognition, surrender, and release of some of the emotional pain connected to the early childhood trauma and wound. This often happens during the Knowledge and Resource and Opening Phases. When you are drifting on a pink cloud, you feel you have arrived in a heavenly place and that from here on out, life will be perfect. While it is a respite from the reality of what is required to dig in and walk the path, it has a purpose. Though spiritually immature, the pink cloud gives you a taste of hope and peace. It is the experience that there is more to life than separation fear and pain.

In the Committed Phase, you are *spiritually maturing*. You walk through life with both feet on the ground, connected to both the reality and the miracle of living. In this place, you have accepted your trauma and wound as one of the conditions of your humanity. Thus, the relationship to your wound changes significantly as you come to understand the purpose of having a wound. Below is a summary of the spiritual purpose and principles of the wound.

Spiritual Purpose and Principles of the Emotional Wound

1. Everyone has an emotional wound. It is part of your spiritual purpose for incarnating.

2. Your wound holds the key to the part of your soul substance that you have come to heal.

3. The consciousness of your wound is the age when

the actual trauma occurred in childhood. If your wound occurred at birth, then the age of your wound is that of a newborn: pre-verbal, sensate, absorbing the ambient environment.

4. Your spiritual work is not to get rid of your wound.

5. Your spiritual work is to receive your wound as a gift; understanding its purpose is to assist in your awakening to the truth of who you are.

6. When spiritually mature, you tend to your wound with compassion, without it dominating your perception and experience of life.

Earlier in our work together, Joyce shared that her birth mother (who was single) had given her up for adoption when Joyce was one year old. She did not have a lot of details except that she had spent several months in an orphanage before being adopted. The couple who adopted her loved her very much, and she grew up in a stable and caring family. Despite this, her early experience of abandonment had left its mark. This mark was Joyce's fear of abandonment and a feeling of helplessness whenever a significant relationship ended or when someone close to her became very ill. During the earlier phases of our work, Joyce had explored her deep fear of being left young and alone, the grief and rage connected to that, and her ongoing fear of abandonment.

Now in the Committed Phase, Joyce could relate to her wound differently. When her wound flared up or was evoked by life experiences or her own thinking, Joyce recognized it both as a felt sense inside her body and as emotional upheaval. When this happened, she would engage in the process of self inquiry, which is part of the Living Practice. When I refer to self inquiry, it is the *inner dialogue of questioning the self.* The Indian Saint Sri Ramana Maharshi was instrumental in developing the process of self inquiry as a path to awakening. This process has been adopted and modified by many disciplines. In my experience, it is one of the most powerful practices that we can utilize to move out of history, into the present moment, and into a greater awareness of Self.

An example of how the process of self inquiry works comes from my own life. I also have a wound of abandonment and helplessness. About fifteen years ago I met a passionate and charismatic man. The fire between us swept me up. He then disappeared just as quickly as he had come into my life, and my wound of helplessness and grief flooded me.

Remember, the *consciousness of the wound* is the age you were when the trauma occurred. So, in that moment my internal emotional reaction was that of a young child. It is important to remember that when your wound is evoked as an adult, 90 percent of your reaction is a reaction to the *past*, not to what is happening *now*.

At the time of this event I was deeply rooted in the Committed Phase, so I knew what to do. I employed the *process of self inquiry*.

The Three Aspects of the Process of Self Inquiry

These three aspects are sometimes referred to as the WAE-Witnessing, Asking and Experiencing. Briefly explained they are:

1) Experiencing—Paying attention to everything you are *experiencing* in the moment (both inside and outside of you).

2) Asking/Questioning—Helps shift you out of your story and back into the present by asking open, unbiased, curious questions. Four essential questions you can choose from to ask yourself: "What's here now?" "What is my unmet need in this moment?" "Who is

the I that is experiencing?" "Who am I?"

3) Witnessing/The Neutral Observer—The God Presence, Pure Consciousness, observing all that is.

It is important to note that we move back and forth through the three aspects while engaged in the inquiry process.

In *Experiencing,* I knew what I was *experiencing*—horrible feelings of dread at the thought of being left alone and forgotten. The room felt dark around me. I could feel my heart pounding, my stomach churning. I wanted to scream and cry. This experience was very familiar. I had felt it many times in my life.

Then I opened to the *Witnessing/Neutral Observer* part of my self. This part knows that your wound is not all encompassing (though the experiencing child consciousness believes it is). This aspect observes *all* that is occurring. It is compassionate, benevolent, peaceful, unattached and sees the wound for what it is: A significant, yet small part of the self. *The Witness/ Neutral Observer is like the sky—seemingly infinite.* It initiates a broader perspective. Much like astronaut Frank Borman's perspective (from the article

"A Science Fiction World—Awesome Forlorn Beauty" in *Life*, 17 January 1969) after he landed the Apollo 8 on the moon. Once there, he had this to say: "The view of the earth from the moon fascinated me—a small disk, 240,000 miles away. It was hard to think that that little thing held so many problems, so many frustrations. Raging nationalistic interests, famines, wars, pestilence, don't show from that distance." We can experience a similar shift in perspective when we get enough distance from our wound by observing it. Observing is not denying. It is fully aware that you are experiencing. *It is simply not attached to what you are experiencing.* The Neutral Observer is the God Presence, the Pure Consciousness that is both the observer and the observed, creator and created.

The aspect, *Asking/Questioning*, patiently helps us come back into the present and objective reality by asking one of the four questions.

I asked myself while experiencing the overwhelming pain inside me, *"What's here now?"* As soon as I asked the question, I began tracking more clearly what was going on inside of me (the felt sense/physical sensations in my body, my thoughts, my emotions) as well as what I was experiencing around me (my environment-observations, sounds, impressions). What I had been experiencing before I began questioning and witnessing, had for the most part, been a historical reaction. Now, the tight hard pain in me began to loosen.

I then asked myself, *"What is my unmet need in this moment?"* As soon as I asked, *I felt* a surge of love for myself. My need was to feel loved and I felt this love just as I asked for it. Most of the time, one's unmet need is immediately actualized as a felt sense in the body, by simply asking the question. Asking/Questioning also invites us to release our limited sense of identity by asking, *"Who is the I that is experiencing?"* or *"Who am I?"* Whenever I had completed noting what I was experiencing while witnessing my experience at the same time, I would repeat one of the four questions. Each time, I allowed the answers to be *felt inside my body*.

I continued this process until I experienced the wound moving from the foreground of my awareness into the background. Through my inquiry, it had dissolved. Nothing outside of me had changed, but everything inside was different. I had moved from the past, from the hurt young child, into the present, the disappointed but thoroughly capable adult. By questioning, "Who is the I that is experiencing?" or "Who am I?", I had also moved from a very limited self-identity to a much broader sense of Self. I had witnessed and understood that the wound is a very small part of the all that I AM. *In that moment, I realized that my wound would no longer have a paralyzing grasp on me. I had learned how to use the tool of self inquiry.*

Joyce also used the process of self inquiry when she found herself unsettled or upset, or when her wound had been activated. One of the results of inquiry in the Committed Phase is that *you learn how to tend to the young hurt part of yourself,* the way a parent soothes a frightened child. You stop judging and trying to get rid of the wound, and instead learn how to comfort the child consciousness of the wound while still being in charge as the adult. This frees you to recognize that you have choices. You are empowered to make decisions from a centered, responsive place.

2. THE NEGATIVE MESSAGES AND BELIEFS

All of us have received negative messages, and all of us have formed negative beliefs based on those messages. The Committed Phase is a game-changer when it comes to how we relate to the messages and beliefs. One change is that we *recognize how negative messages and beliefs cluster together, and how they are connected to the misconceptions that lie within the wound, that we have come to heal.*

I asked Joyce what sort of negative messages she had received that she felt had marked her life. Joyce shared that she had always been very good at math. She had tested out of basic math in junior high school and had been elevated to an honors course in seventh grade. "That's great," I said. "Not great," Joyce replied, "when the kids around you start calling you nerd and refuse to have lunch with you. I spent many lunch hours sitting by myself. It was quite lonely." "What belief did you create from that experience?" I asked.

"Oh, it was clear. I didn't fit in, and since I wasn't like the other kids, my belief was that I'm different and this is wrong." This message and belief ran like a river through her life.

Parental Messages

This one was easy for Joyce. Her earliest message, "You're not like the other kids," landed inside her when her biological mother left her at an orphanage. Since most kids are kept by their birth parents, being abandoned meant she wasn't like other kids. Her adoptive parents worked hard to compensate for that early childhood experience. Despite that, Joyce believed their trying so hard really meant she wasn't like the other kids. Strike two.

Societal Messages

"Wow," Joyce said, "There is a lot to that one. After my parents adopted me, they had two of their own children. My brother and sister have brown skin and jet-black hair just like my parents, and I'm white and blond. I can't tell you how many people would stare at me whenever my family was together. They would ask my parents for details about me. Most of the time, my parents would just ignore them, but sometimes they would get angry and pull me away from the staring eyes." Strike three. "I felt strange when people stared. I believed there was something odd or wrong in being different. Just like my being good in math was wrong somehow."

Self-Generated Messages

Joyce felt that it was wrong to be different. The message she had been telling herself was that she didn't fit in. This often created an experience of feeling alone and that cemented both the message and her belief. Until she reached the Committed Phase, she thought that being different was a negative.

As stated before, the Committed Phase is a game-changer. Before this phase, your life is heavily influenced by the Five Obstacles. They have become part of your identity. In the Committed Phase, you are finally able to put negative messages and beliefs into a mature perspective. You've come to realize that messages and beliefs are untrue and that they are psychological misunderstandings. *You also realize that messages and beliefs are part of the transformational process that is taking place.* We are born, and we take on an emotional wound to help us discover and then heal, the part of our soul's substance that is still separated from the truth of who we are. Messages and beliefs form part of the constellation we have come to heal. You could almost say that the messages and beliefs hold the opposite of the truth of who you are. For example, if a message/belief you received is that there is something wrong with you, you have come to learn that there is nothing wrong with you. Another example might be if your message/ belief is that you are unlovable, you have come to learn that you are completely lovable.

Therefore, in this phase, you consciously take up the practice of uncovering and healing the misconceptions that have arisen out of the negative messages and beliefs.

3. DEFENSES AND JUDGING

In the Committed Phase, you become acutely aware of how much of your life is and has been spent in reaction, judging, and defense. As you may recall, defense systems certainly have their rightful place. They are instinctive and designed to keep us safe from harm. In this phase, you are aware of when you are in defense, what it feels like, and what the "trigger" was that activated your defense. Added to this is the awareness that most triggers are not real. We come to realize that, in fact, *most triggers are our very own projections.*

As Joyce discovered this, she could let go of defending when there was no real threat. In one session, I asked her to give me a recent example of this in her life. "Okay," she said. "Since I have been paying attention to defenses, I have been surprised by how much I defend." "That's great," I said, "people are defending a lot of the time, but they are not aware of it—so this is wonderful." When she heard this, she looked relieved. "Well," she said, "Just yesterday I took my dog to the pet store to get some food. He likes to go with me, and I love our little outings. The line at the register was long, and there were lots of people with their dogs. My dog is a mixed breed—he has long ears, a long body, and short legs. The woman in front of me had a statuesque greyhound with her, and she looked back at Jep (my dog's name) and snickered. My body became stiff and I sneered at both her and her dog as I went into defense. It was as if I had been personally threatened. I looked down at Jep, and he was just wagging his tail at the woman, as if she had looked at him in friendship. I realized how ridiculous it was for me to defend against something that wasn't threatening or real. I started to laugh, and in that moment, I felt kindness toward this woman who I assumed had scorned Jep. I realized she was just like me. She judged, I defended, different sides of the same coin. I felt so grateful for that experience."

As I listened to Joyce, I knew with certainty she was on her way to becoming free, free to live the light of truth that is her essence and the essence of all creation.

4. BELIEVING YOUR STORY IS ALL THERE IS

> "I am not what happened to me,
> I am what I choose to become."
> —C.G. Jung,
> *Memories, Dreams, Reflections*

By this time, you are well on your way to being freed from believing that your story is the master of your destiny. Before this phase, your sense of self and path in life had been governed by your story—the external events and facts that have made up the passage of time. Now, you approach your story almost as a continuing mythological blueprint for the journey of your soul. Earlier life experiences (the story), as well as the stories you are making up every day based on limiting beliefs, are now accepted as the "breadcrumbs" scattered intentionally along the path. You understand that these "breadcrumbs" are intended to help you find your way back to the wholeness of yourself. In this phase, you *utilize your stories to learn discernment.* The ability to discern empowers you to choose what you want to become and how you want to live your life.

This in no way minimizes experiences of pain, disappointment, and loss. The Committed Phase teaches that these experiences are inescapable factors of being human. I cannot tell you how many people I have worked with who have asked when will they receive the "prize" of no more wound, pain, or disappointment. They are looking outside themselves for some escape from their story because they still believe their story is the controlling factor of their lives.

I too, thought like that at the beginning of my journey. In the Committed Phase, *you deeply understand what it means to be on the path to awakening.* Believing your story is the truth has moved into the realm of STORY. In other words, while useful, you know it's fiction—it cannot define the truth of who you are.

In this phase, Joyce felt liberated in relationship to her story. She had come to understand that *all her life experiences were sacred.* They were there to help her become the conscious co-creator of her life. One day we sat and talked about this. I asked her how she felt about being left by her birth mother, then adopted, about having blond hair and white skin instead of black hair and brown skin, and being considered different by strangers and classmates. She said, "What I have learned is that at the very heart of all of us, we are not that different. We all want to be loved and accepted just the way we are. My 'story' has become my teacher. Whenever I find myself caught up in believing it, I slow down, go inside, and feel the truth deep inside my heart."

As she shared this, I sat there marveling at this young woman. She had arrived at an essential point of spiritual maturation. *Maturation knows there is nothing to get rid of;*

the only change needed is perspective. Scratch the surface of any human and you will find love and light—the same truth that exists in you also exists in them. More accurately, it is not scratching the surface of another that is needed. What is needed is removing the stain of misunderstanding from your own perception that has prevented you from seeing the truth to begin with.

5. BELIEVING YOUR THOUGHTS

The final frontier or obstacle that separates you from the direct experience of the truth of who you are is in believing your thoughts. In the Committed Phase, you are engaged in the dance of *sometimes you believe your thoughts and sometimes you don't.* The difference is that even when you find yourself believing them, you also have the subtle awareness that thoughts are not real. You are waking up from the dream!

You are connecting the dots between what you think and how you feel. You understand how thoughts create emotions. Joyce shared with me how each day had become a kind of game—an opportunity for her to practice observing her thoughts and the accompanying emotions. Joyce set the game up like this: She would intentionally think a thought and feel the emotion that followed. Then she would intentionally distance herself from the thought by simply witnessing it. As she did this she would experience the emotion lessen, dissolve and settle into peace. She was thrilled with her discovery! In your spiritual maturation, you can disarm the drama your thoughts are often creating simply by not giving them power. This supports you in being able to move your thoughts, story, defenses, messages, beliefs, and wounds from the *foreground of your life experience into the background*, where they are no longer the dominating factor. This is true power!

In turn, the radiant background, the typically elusive Divine Presence/Pure Consciousness (light, love, joy, and peace—the truth of who you are and all that is) moves into the foreground of your awareness. *This awareness then becomes your dominant perception and experience.*

My first spiritual teacher, Swami Muktananda, taught that the mind is either your worst enemy or your greatest friend. In *Where are You Going* he wrote that the mind is "the source of our bondage or liberation." He was speaking about our proclivity to let negative thinking and our attachment to a narrow sense of self-identity run our lives, producing unhappiness and dissatisfaction. Through his teachings, I learned about the power of the mind. Instead of feeding the "monkey mind," I learned that we can train the mind to help us awaken to the truth of who we are. This is done by not believing the runaway train of our constant, uncontrolled, unceasing thoughts that create and sustain our stories. In the Committed Phase, as we distance ourselves from believing our thoughts, the mind becomes quiet. It is then receptive to the peaceful presence of the Illuminated Self.

Another one of my spiritual teachers, Emilie Conrad, who founded *Continuum*, posed this question for inquiry: "How can we live in a system without being bound by it?" In other words, we live in cultures that have systems designed to make things run smoothly, according to cultural beliefs. All too often, however, we let those systems define who we are. And all too often, our collective approach to these systems is based on cynicism and fear. Each of us has contributed to humanity's collective creations. To free yourself to live in the world with the support of functioning systems, without letting them define or deaden you, requires that you become free of pessimistic and damaging thoughts. To achieve this, you need to begin creating space between your thoughts. You need to pause and *s-l-o-w d-o-w-n* so that you can experience your bright Self. This in turn opens you to the *River of Peace*, a flowing stillness that exists within you and all creation. Your direct experience of this gently releases you from the obstacles. *Your Awakened Self is emerging.*

In this phase, you begin glimpsing that life is a dream and the mind is making everything up, projecting thoughts onto the world. *This brings up the fundamental question of "What is real?"* Prior to the Committed Phase, one often has a ferocious hold on what they are convinced is reality. This conviction is anchored in the belief that the obstacles (wounds, messages, belief systems, defenses, stories, thoughts) are *the* reality.

Now, committed to doing the work, reality is turned upside down, and it's okay. In fact, it is enlivening. You welcome wonder and questioning. There is a lightening within you as you let go of believing the thoughts that previously were the determining factor of not only your life, but of all reality.

> *"One bird sits still Watching the work of God..."*
> —Thomas Merton, *A Book of Hours*

The Committed Phase in Conclusion

In the earlier phases, your fears made it difficult to question and tolerate anything or anyone different from your own narrow worldview. Fear creates a world of assumptions. What a relief to becoming free of this. *People would fall to their knees kissing every being a thousand times over if they experienced the truth of who they are.* In the Committed Phase, you are receiving glimpses of this truth and thus finding it easier to accept all and to love.

You are also better skilled at tolerating the unknown, because your sense of safety and identity is rooted deep inside the Self. You are now better equipped to be with what is occurring in the moment. In fact, you may even relish playing in the realm of the unknown, the arising moment of NOW. This is far different from the beginning phases, when safety is only possible by demanding to know the reasons and the outcome in order to be with what is happening—as if such a thing were possible! Indeed, in the Committed Phase, you know that a specific outcome is never guaranteed.

You have *engaged life as the living practice.* This is the longest phase in the Remembering Sequence until you arrive home, realized in the Self. You are preparing the ground to receive Grace, with her sweet surrender in the Illumination Phase.

The Committed Phase is developing your capacity for patience and compassion. It is cultivating your faith. It is refining your ability to discern and respond. It is teaching you the wisdom of your unique path. It is helping you to embrace the perfect, divine timing of *your* awakening to the truth of who you are.

CHAPTER #10

The Key Points to Committed

1. You have embraced life as the classroom for your awakening.
2. You engage life as your living practice.
3. Each day has become a new opportunity to practice creating, experiencing, pause, inquiry, and transforming.
4. You commit to the work of uncovering and healing your misconceptions intrinsic to the obstacles.
5. The Process of Self Inquiry/The WAE and its three aspects (Experiencing, Asking/Questioning, Witnessing/Neutral Observer) play a key role in the Committed Phase.
6. Your relationship to your wound changes.
7. You understand that your wound's spiritual purpose is to heal the part of your soul substance that is still separated from the truth of who you are.
8. You realize that your wound, defenses, beliefs, thoughts, messages, and repetitive stories are clustered together as a constellation. This is done to help signal and clarify for you what you have come to heal. You recognize your primary misconception.

9. Your wound, defenses, story, thoughts, and belief systems move from the foreground to the background of your experience and perception of life.
10. You understand that everyone is co-creating his or her life unconsciously or consciously.
11. You understand that becoming a conscious co-creator is one of the gifts of being human.
12. You understand that free will is another gift of being human.
13. You are no longer the victim of circumstances.
14. You are aware that you always have choices.
15. There is no one left to blame.
16. You are completely responsible for your life.
17. You realize how much time you spend judging yourself and others and how automatically you defend.
18. You are spiritually maturing.
19. You no longer lament why difficult things happen but seek ways to remain present and responsive.
20. You are learning how to move from reacting to life (the past) to discerning and responding to life (the present moment of now).
21. Spiritual maturation accepts that there is nothing to get rid of and that the only change needed is your perspective.

22. Each experience becomes a sacred invitation to awaken.

23. You are learning how to distance yourself from believing that your thoughts and stories are the ultimate reality.

24. You are learning the powerful connection between your thoughts and your emotions.

25. Your mind begins to experience a quiet stillness, and you have moments of illuminated peace.

26. You practice dissolving your assumptions.

27. As you cultivate the Witness/Neutral Observer presence, you are beginning to see that life is a dream that your mind and the collective mind are creating.

28. You are becoming comfortable with the unknown.

29. The Committed Phase is the longest phase in the Remembering Sequence until you are firmly established in the Illumination Phase.

30. You are preparing the ground for Grace in the Illumination Phase.

31. Your Awakened Self is slowly emerging.

THE LIVING PRACTICE #10
Committed

Creating, Experiencing, Pause, Inquiry, and Transformation

You may want to periodically revisit these questions as you journey the Committed Phase of your path.
Find a quiet place for contemplation to consider and write about the following:

1. What fears (if any) do you have about the Committed Phase?

2. What excites you about the Committed Phase?

3. What parts of your life are you consciously co-creating?

4. What parts of your life would you like to become more conscious about?

5. Is there anyone you still blame for certain events or situations in your life? Write about this. If yes, can you feel how you give away your power to consciously co-create when you blame? Write about this.

6. How has your relationship to your wound, defenses, messages, beliefs, your story, and your thoughts changed as you have progressed through the phases?

7. What would you like to focus on healing regarding the obstacles in the Committed Phase?

8. Choose one aspect of your life that you would like to actively engage with as the focus of your living practice. The purpose is to broaden your understanding of your participation as co-creator. So, choose one aspect to specifically focus on creating, experiencing, pause, inquiry, and transforming. Write about your experience of the process of choosing and what you are learning by applying the Living Practice.

Inward Journey to Observe Your Thoughts and Quiet the Mind

Find a comfortable place to lie or sit down. Close your eyes and focus on your breathing, noticing the state of your breathing... You might discover that your breath is shallow or fast or anxious or deep or quiet. After discovering the quality of your breathing, take three long, slow, deep breaths with the intention to open and relax your body and your mind... If you are already relaxed, this will support you dropping even deeper into an opened state of awareness.

With your next breath, imagine that you are walking up a hill, a hill that overlooks a tranquil blue lake. As you ascend the hill, you are occupied with thinking about everything you have done today and everything you think you need to do tomorrow... You have had a very busy day. Random thoughts about past events surface, ones that remain active and incomplete... Your mind is racing back and forth from past to future. You find yourself reacting emotionally to your various thoughts. One moment you might feel sad or anxious, and in the next moment you might feel satisfied or hopeful. Your feelings bounce back and forth in reaction to your thoughts.... You are not aware of your surroundings because your thoughts occupy the rental space in your mind...

Now, you have reached the top of the hill. Your mind is still busy with runaway thoughts, many of them negative, and your emotions continue to react. In the middle of a thought, you look down and see grass beneath your feet. It's so green... It looks soft and inviting. You decide to sit... Once seated you look out and see the blue lake below you... You look up and see a very clear blue sky... The air is warm. There is a fragrant breeze casting the scent of oregano and lavender in your direction... You look around for the source and notice that the hill is dotted with herbs. As you slowly breathe in their medicinal qualities, you feel your body relax.... You are slowing down, pausing, being with what it is here. As you naturally relax, you realize that you have not been thinking. Instead, you have *been immersed in the sensate fullness* of the natural world.... With this awareness, you decide to practice simply observing the working of your mind and thoughts. Relaxed, you begin watching your thoughts as they arise, as if they are off in the distance, little dreams floating above the lake... You sit quietly on the hill observing them... Your thoughts are losing power; they are surrendering the grasp they had on you just a few minutes ago... As your thoughts let go, your emotional state softens. The longer you simply witness them, the more peaceful you become... You are at rest and so is your mind... Your mind is serene, just like the still blue lake below you. When a thought surfaces, you simply witness it float across the lake and vanish.

With your mind still, thoughts no longer have the power to interrupt your peaceful state. You are experiencing the eternal, quiet radiance of Illuminated Presence. You are experiencing the truth of who you are...

You sit here on the hill breathing and being breathed, life flowing through you as you. In this state, there is nowhere to go and there is nothing to do...

Gently bringing this inward journey to a close, focus again on your breath… Slowly open your eyes, and when you are ready, sit up. Spend some time writing about your experience of the journey. In particular, you may want to write about what it was like to observe your thoughts in the distance and your felt experience of being free of them.

Gently take in your surroundings before you stand up and go about the rest of your day.

An Affirmation of Support in the Committed Phase

"I welcome all of my life as the sacred path for my awakening. I welcome my spiritual maturation. I know that the Illuminated Eternal Presence is watching over me, loving me, every step of the way."

11

PHASE 7:
ILLUMINATION

*"When you have started to awaken
and see that there are other planes of reality
that are equally valid to the one
which presently exists, you learn
how to live more or less with
more and more planes simultaneously,
which is what freedom is about.
It's not totally standing in one plane,
it's not standing anywhere at all."*

—RAM DASS

In 1985, having overcome an earlier life-threatening illness and having embraced the path of awakening, I found myself cast down into despair again. A short-lived marriage had become a nightmare—plagued by my husband's alcoholism, my codependency, and his abusive behavior. I had gone from heaven to hell in a matter of months. We had married in May, and now, in the following autumn I was filing for separation. He was in a rehab halfway house, his third attempt at sobriety within five months.

I was totally lost. I wondered how I could have fallen so quickly from the place of pure joy I had been in at the time of our meeting. On this particularly cold day, I decided to attend a one-day workshop presented by Siddha Yoga called "The Power of the Mind." It was at a lovely center I had been going to for a few years to meditate. The small group was gathered in the basement, and the presenter spoke briefly about the mind's capacity to be either a tool for transformation or a weapon for destruction. It all depended, he shared, on *your intention and ability to focus the mind on the truth, rather than the illusions produced by the mind's continuous stream of thoughts.*

After his short speech, we sat together to chant and meditate. We began chanting a very loving mantra. One of the purposes of the chant was to feed the mind's incessant need for thoughts. After all, that is what the mind does—it thinks. Giving the mind something loving and kind to focus on, such as chanting, helps release the vise-grip that our random, chaotic, and often unkind thoughts have on us. Chanting sacred words holds and transmits the high vibration of truth. Repetition of those words helps to replace our negative tapes with kind ones while the resonance of truth soothes the mind, body, emotions, and soul. On that day, we chanted the words, *Om Namah Shivaya*. Translated into English, it means, "I bow to Shiva, the supreme reality, the Inner Self, the Pure Consciousness that is the essence of all." In other words, the truth of who you are!

During the initial chanting, I felt a torrent of emotion. I was caught up in the angry thoughts that I could not stop thinking and subsequently feel. I kept thinking, "How could I have lost myself after so much hard work? I'm so stupid. I am not worth anything. I'll never get better. I hate myself." With those thoughts came feelings of anger, grief, and shame. I was in sheer torture with my violent thoughts and feelings. I could find no way out of this terrible state. In the midst of this insanity, I kept repeating the mantra that was being sung by the group around me as well as by myself.

After about an hour of chanting, something totally unexpected occurred. In one moment I was trapped by despairing thoughts and feelings, and in the next I was transported into absolute freedom. *I was experiencing the Grace of Illumination.* It is impossible for words to transmit my experience. I can only describe what it was like in me. *I had come back from hell to heaven in the space of one breath.*

I sat there in perfect harmony and peace. My mind had become tranquil and clear. I was Pure Consciousness. My body was as light as a feather. In fact, I was sublimely aware that while I sat in a body, this body was not *me*. It was too small to contain all the "I" that I am. The "I" that I am exists within all of creation. Therefore, the "I" *is* all of creation. I saw an ethereal light in the heart within the body I inhabited, radiating out into the world.

Everywhere I looked, this same light glowed in everyone and everything. My heart felt absolute, unquestionable love for all. I experienced a profound peace, flowing like a river. This river of peace moved through and connected all creation as one. Within this peace arose a humbled joy for the miracle of all life.

The veil of separation and duality that existed before had dissolved and here I was, at one, in total communion. There had ceased to be a separate me. A piece that I have written, titled *Ulysses Revisited,* explores the dissolution of the veil and in its place, the Awakened Self as the One who sees all:

> *"My eyes were gently opened and I was made to see.*
> *I looked across the milky universe and then spiraled*
> *down into the mouth of a shark, swallowing a small,*
> *silver fish whose eye still shone with life.*
> *I looked up and orbited a village that was dark and quiet.*
> *A star flew across the sky and winked at me.*
> *I saw a mother hit her child and then I blinked and*
> *saw her kissing him. The more I looked, the more*
> *my vision cleared. I saw light—everywhere.*
> *It was brilliant. It shone in everything and*
> *everyone—even the hand that had hit the child,*
> *though not bright, still held light."*

As I sat there gently watching life, I saw that *life* as we believe it to be is really a dream, a figment of our mind. The "I" within me lovingly observed everything that was happening without the slightest ripple of fear or attachment.

In this place, I understood that *the idea of separation* is simply a misunderstanding that arises out of the negative belief that a separate identity is necessary for survival. This is a belief that has been collectively held and promoted by humanity.

Now, *released from the dream,* I was awake to the truth of who I am and the truth within everyone. I remember sitting there looking out at the world from this new vantage point of pure awareness. I was the observer and the observed. I could see for thousands of miles since there was no *me* to limit my experience.

Across the earth and out into the vast universe I saw a radiating, brilliant light. I sat there in rapture and gratitude. I was not grateful for being released from my previous suffering. In this state, I neither felt nor remembered suffering. I was simply grateful. I was in awe of the miraculous moment. There was no past and no future. I understood that there is no pain to be released from, and I came to understand that suffering and desperation do not exist in the Illuminated state. This does not mean that physical pain does not exist. It simply means that the emotional and mental suffering we often attach to pain does not exist.

In fact, nothing exists except for the "I am" Pure Consciousness in the moment. I was quietly *grateful for the unfolding miracle that I experienced in each second.* I now knew that EVERYONE and EVERYTHING is a miracle that is being expressed and witnessed moment to moment by God, Pure Consciousness, Spirit, Source, the Universal Presence. I understood that there is no "out there." In the words of Alan Watts, "You are an aperture through which the universe is looking at and exploring itself."

Eventually, the day's workshop was over. I stood up, put on my coat, and went on my way. The experience of Illumination, however, stayed with me. Wherever I went and whomever I met, I saw only the expression of love pouring out of them and me. Even when I saw people "quarreling," I recognized it as confusion, a clumsy attempt at expressing love for each other. My heart felt only the steady beat of joy and the pervasive peace connecting all creation as one.

Each night I went to sleep Illuminated, and each morning I woke up in the same state. *Past and future had ceased to exist in me.* I was in love with the miracle that each moment—*the Now*—ceaselessly offers us. Thus, experience was not being measured in me by time, though I was aware of the movement of it. I understood that

Illumination is ever-present, though we may not be tapped into the awareness of it. The days and nights passed in sweet oneness.

Seven days later, as I sat at the dining table eating the miracle of the food before me, my experience of Illumination dissolved. It left as quickly as it had come. I was back in the experience of duality. I felt slightly separate. With that, a little fear arose in me as I looked outside of myself, feeling myself separate from the rest of life around me. The thoughts in my mind slowly began pulling at me, and while part of me *still knew* they weren't real, part of me began to believe them again.

Since that week, *which I have treasured as a supreme gift of Grace*, I have had moments, hours, even days of experiencing the absolute Illuminating truth of who I am and all that is. I have not, however, sustained this awareness to the degree I did during that week in 1985.

Over the years, I have wondered why I did not remain awakened, and the passage of time has taught me three important characteristics intrinsic to receiving the Illumination Phase. These characteristics are *Without Demand, Grace,* and *Spiritual Maturation: The Temporary and Established Illumination State.*

WITHOUT DEMAND

The first characteristic involves commitment by the seeker. As you know, the work of the sixth phase of human consciousness is the Committed Phase. Your commitment is served by doing the work *without demanding a result*. You can demand, of course. You have freewill. I have thrown a tantrum or two when, in a fit of frustration or agony of not wanting to be with "what is," I demand to wake up. The demand of not wanting to be present with "what is" is the antithesis of Illumination. Illumination is completely being with "what is" in every single moment. Needless to say, demanding hasn't worked, because the path to Illumination is not designed to acquiesce to the whims and follies of the unstable mind, negative limited ego and personality. Rather, it is designed to follow the wisdom of your soul, which, aligned with God/Spirit, is guiding you home to the truth of who you are. *Awakening is an alchemical event.* Your true nature is revealed to you in precisely the right moment and not a second sooner or later.

GRACE

The second characteristic is Grace. I have designated Grace as a proper noun, because for me, Grace is a holy being. Grace is the active messenger sent to bestow blessings, to intercede on your behalf in moments of crisis, and to awaken the seeker. If God or Pure Consciousness is the Creator and Generator, Grace is its willing transmitter. Like the Fairy Godmother who, with one wave of her wand, turns a pumpkin into a golden carriage, Grace in the space of one divine breath gifts the seeker with Illumination. Similarly, in Abrahamic religions, the Holy Spirit, often referred to as the voice of God, the divine force, or creative spirit, is Grace the messenger, the active principle, with the ability to bestow gifts on behalf of God. The *New Oxford American Dictionary* defines Grace in part as, "The free and unmerited favor of God." Thus, it is benevolent Grace who casts the light of awareness into the heart and mind of the seeker, clearing away the obstacles caught in the shadows of forgetting.

SPIRITUAL MATURATION:
The Temporary and Established Illuminated State

The third characteristic I have come to understand regards your ability to maintain the state of Illumination. Awakening and remaining awake are gradual processes that require spiritual maturation. *Being consciously engaged in this process is the fundamental purpose of this book.* I have used multiple words to describe it, such as remembering, returning, healing, transforming, awakening, and maturing. In this process, you are clearing the obstacles that have blocked the way of Illumination.

You are holy. You are the light. You always have been and always will be. Like most of humanity, you have just forgotten. By virtue of being on the path, you are being made ready for this realized state. You cannot willfully hold on to Illumination. It comes and goes. You are maturing through its coming and going. These movements of consciousness, remembering-forgetting-remembering, are not only clearing you. *They are tempering you with an increased resiliency to be with it all,* to be responsive, present, and appreciative for all of life's experiences. The "I AM" awareness is growing in you. As written earlier, Swami Muktananda said, "Grace is ever-present, always pouring itself into you; you just can't hold it yet." Spiritual maturation is developing the ability to hold the gift of Illumination given to you through Grace.

What brings us out of the Illumination state? Fear. Conscious or not, it is your personality's fear of the loss of yourself as a distinct or separate being and a belief that your identity/sense of self can only be maintained by separation. This fear is maintained by the negative limited ego. As you mature, fears lessen and a sense of the whole Self, the "I Am" Pure Consciousness expands.

In my own spiritual maturation process, I have reached the stage where I am fully aware that while a small part of my personality still believes in separation and the illusion of duality, the greater part of me, the "I am," is very aware of Illumination. I feel its constant presence within me. I live knowing that I am experiencing the dream of being human with a slight felt sense of separation. At the same time, I am experiencing the "I Am" Pure Consciousness, observing all and being the observed from an unchangeable state of peaceful awareness.

REMEMBER

That week of Illumination in 1985 has brought me many gifts. One of the gifts is that an imprint of that holy experience lives on in me. Another gift is that I can share this experience with others as a way of giving hope, to help them remember. For those who thirst for the truth, it is helpful to hear about other people's experiences. It confirms that such a possibility exists for everyone.

As you live your life and move through the various phases, relating and learning from the obstacles that appear to stand between you and the truth of who you are, trust this: Obstacles are meant to help open and heal you. Clearing them is part of the work of remembering. Remembering, helps you find your way home to Illumination.

When I recall that brittle fall day, being at one of the lowest points in my life when all signs seemed to shout, "You are no good, give up, you will not progress," I am reminded of Grace. It was in that place of despair that I was met by truth, lifted by Spirit, and given a taste of its sweetness. *I bring their message back to you: Do not despair, you are never alone. Persevere. You will be brought back to the Illuminated beauty within you and within all of creation.* For this lighted truth, while elusive, lives within you. It is you.

In those moments when you are visited by Grace and opened to a direct experience of the Illumination Phase, the Five Obstacles will cease to exist. From this vantage point, you will have understood their purpose. You will also see that they have been part of an elaborate dream you have awoken from, at least for the moment. In Hinduism, this dream is called Maya. Maya is the totality of all mental projections, unreal, but believed to be real. Humans are typically caught in believing that the dream/Maya, duality/separation is the only reality. Thus, in the beginning phases, we tend to believe the obstacles as if they are the truth of who we are. In the Illumination Phase, *we see them as illusions*, the play of consciousness, Maya. We accept that obstacles are part of the divine play. In the Illumination Phase, everything is a delight, even the obstacles.

> *"And could you keep your heart in wonder*
> *at the daily miracles of your life, your pain*
> *would not seem less wondrous than your joy."*
> —Kahlil Gibran, The Prophet

A child in its opened state lights up in the moment—something new to discover, to feel and experience, without predetermination or judgment. With the purity of a child and an adult's ability of awareness, each moment then becomes a state of wonder. Every moment and therefore EVERY experience is met by you with a YES!

Moments of Illumination are what I call *"spiritual carrots."* God, Spirit, in its infinite love through Grace, bestows moments of Illumination on the seeker as a way of saying, "This is the way, keep going! You are almost there!"

When you fall out of Illumination back into a sense of separation, these experiences will be your joyful reminder of the truth within you. As you stay committed, the journey back and forth across the Illumination threshold becomes an integrated part of your path. You welcome it when it arises and gently accept it when it leaves.

One day, when you are having an Awakened experience of the truth of who you are, perhaps *that* is the day you become established in the sublime state of Pure Consciousness-Illumination.

CHAPTER #11

The Key Points to Illumination

1. Illumination: Awakened, Self-Realized, the "I Am," Enlightened, Nirvana. It is the state of Pure Consciousness, the state of Pure Awareness.

2. As Pure Consciousness, the seeker established in the Illumination State experiences the ineffable, unchangeable state of awareness.

3. In this state, you are seamlessly the observer and the observed.

4. Illumination is perceived as light, expressed as love, experienced as joy and peace. It is the truth of who you are and all that is.

5. Illumination lives in the present moment.

6. Illumination has no past or future.

7. Illumination accepts that all is. Period.

8. Illumination is free of the attachment of anything being other than it is or anyone being other than they are.

9. Illumination usually comes and goes as a glimpse or in a moment when the mind becomes quiet and your identification as a separate self has dissolved.

10. Preparation for Illumination requires your intention to commit to doing the work without demanding or expecting to be "rewarded" by awakening, by becoming Illuminated. In other words, let go....

11. Spiritual maturation is usually a gradual process—in part, experiencing temporary states of Illumination—creating resiliency within the seeker.

12. Grace awakens Illumination in the seeker.

13. Preparation includes training the mind to focus on the truth rather than illusions, which are the projections of a chaotic mind.

14. If you were to fell a tree in the forest, which stroke is the one that brings the tree down? Is it the first, the tenth, the 100th or the final stroke? Each stroke plays its part in felling the tree. The same is true for each moment lived, each breath breathed. Each has an integral part in Illuminating, awakening, in returning you to the truth of who you are.

15. Each moment that you experience Illumination, you are forever changed.

16. Fear, a belief/sense of separation, is what disrupts the Illumination state.

17. I am not in charge of when I will have the direct experience of awakening. Neither are you.

18. Eventually, each person will awaken and stay awake in the truth. When will that be? I have no idea.

19. Do the work of awakening and hold it lightly. Surrender...

20. Your task is to trust that Spirit/God/Pure Consciousness in its infinite wisdom is taking care of you and all that is.

21. All is well and in perfect Divine order.

THE LIVING PRACTICE #11
Illumination

Creating, Experiencing, Pause, Inquiry, and Transformation

Find a quiet place for contemplation to consider and write about the following:

1. What did you resonate the most with in reading this chapter?

2. What questions arose in you?

3. What doubts do you have?

4. Do you recall moments in your life of being in the Illumination state?

5. If yes, write about your experience of them.

6. If you do not recall any experiences of Illumination, what is this like for you?

7. What are your personal greatest tools or gifts on your path now? For example, have you developed patience or faith?

8. What are your personal impediments at this time on your path? For example, impatience and negative thinking.

9. What are your thoughts about Grace?

10. Where do you feel a demand in yourself, in your life?

11. What fears do you have about awakening?

Inward Journey to Open to Grace and the Illumination State of Pure Consciousness

Find a comfortable place to sit or lie down. Close your eyes and focus on your breathing, noticing the state of your breathing... You might discover that your breath is shallow or fast or anxious or deep or quiet. After discovering the quality of your breathing, take three long, slow, deep breaths with the intention to open and relax your body and your mind... If you are already relaxed, this will support you dropping even deeper into an opened state of awareness.

With your next breath, imagine that you are being transported to a place of your choosing where you feel safe and happy. It might be a deep, green, pine forest, a meadow filled with bright flowers, or the edge of the ocean with dolphins playing in the distance.... Give yourself some time to discover the perfect place for you to be and rest for a while....

Once you have arrived in your special place, pause, take time to see, hear, taste, smell, and feel the beautiful surroundings....

Eventually you become aware that by focusing on *experiencing* your surroundings rather than thinking about them, you have become one with them. You are no longer separate from the trees, the wind, or the water. Instead, you are having the experience of being of all this beauty. In this moment, you are quietly aware that *you are* the rustle of wind... *you are* the branches being moved by the wind... *you are* the sound of water in the distance, *you are* the sweet taste of the bubbling brook... *you are* the warmth of the sun, *you are* the bird flying overhead, *you are* the person experiencing all of this right now...*You are* the light that radiates from your heart touching the wind, trees, water, sun, and birds, just as *you are* their light that is touching you... *You are* the observer, watching all of this happen, and *you are* the one being observed....You are Pure Consciousness, creating, experiencing, and perceiving itself... Grace in her easy way has Awakened you to this wonder... In this moment, you understand the truth of who you are and all that is, perceived as light, expressed as love, experienced as joy and peace...Pause, take time to deeply experience this precious state.

Gently bringing this inward journey to a close, focus again on your breath... Slowly open your eyes, and when you are ready, sit up. Spend some time writing about your experience of the journey. In particular, you may want to write about what it felt like to be one with everything and what it was like to be the observer and the observed at the same time.

Gently take in your surroundings before you stand up and go about the rest of your day.

An Affirmation of Support in the Illumination Phase:

"I am the light, the love, the joy, the peace. I am Pure Consciousness. This is the truth of who I am and all that is. I bow in gratitude for this knowledge, Illuminated in me through Grace."

PART THREE
Here You Are

12

CONSCIOUSLY CO-CREATING YOUR LIFE THROUGH THE LIVING PRACTICE

"We are not going in circles,

we are going upwards.

The path is a spiral;

we have already climbed

many steps."

—HERMANN HESSE, SIDDHARTHA

Do you remember back to the beginning, when you first opened this book? Something compelled you to read it and to engage in the living practice of remembering the truth of who you are. Your study and practice have opened you to a greater degree of consciousness and most likely a more opened heart. It has set you on the path of self-understanding, of awakening. What an extraordinary gift it is to be human, and a consciously co-creating one!

Now here you are, in the last chapter. The knowledge and insights you have gained can serve you for the rest of your life, as your journey of awakening continues. Ultimately, all *knowledge and awareness comes down to integrating it into your daily life*. The gift in becoming the conscious co-creator of your life is that you get to embrace each day as the Living Practice of Creating, Experiencing, Pause, Inquiry, and Transformation. Now, *you* have the tools to live your gift of being human effectively, opened to life.

I understand how enticing it would be to take this book as a straight, linear formula when you try to apply it. (First I need to do this...then this.) I know that when we are hurting, we want fast answers and quick relief—anything to be out of pain and suffering. That longing for relief can create a demand within us. That demand could be to work from Phase 1—Sleepwalking to absolute fulfillment in the Illumination of Phase 7, with the belief that you will never go back to the earlier phases or fall into the obstacles, ever again. But just as water does not flow in a straight line, neither does life. Water meanders and curves, dips and rises on its journey. So, too, it is most likely to be for you on your journey home to the truth of who you are.

But now there is a significant difference from when you began this book. Now you have the knowledge of awareness, heart-opening experiences of the truth, and the perseverance of commitment.

Let's look again at the principles of the Living Practice that are intrinsic to the gift of being human. These are the tools that will help you continue to grow, open and remember the truth of who you are.

1. CREATING:
The Act of Planting and Tending the Seeds of Your Creations

You are co-creating every moment of your life. Co-creating means that you are always in creative partnership with Source, connected to all that is, whether conscious of this or not. When one deeply understands the interconnectedness of all life, that in and of itself is a miraculous awakening. I spent some time in Uganda. While there I got to go into the 'bush' with a naturalist guide. He explained how the Whistling Acacia tree is protected from herbivores such as Giraffes and Elephants by having a symbiotic relationship with stinging ants. The tree provides nuts as shelter for the ants while the ants sting those animals who would try to eat the tree. Thus, the tree is preserved and the ants have a home. This is one tiny example of our interconnected world. So much for life being random and meaningless, as some would have you believe. Everything and everyone has a purpose. Including you! Open, look around you. Everything and everyone you see is connected. *You are creating this world together!*

Understanding the depth of the gift you've been given by having a human life, gives you direct access to consciously co-create your life. This is true power. True power requires wisdom, love and responsibility. Everything you create, effects everything. As you live more consciously, you are wise to the intentions underneath your seeds of creation.

Now, with more self-awareness, you can discern when you are positively aligned with a creation—You are holding an intention connected with your true purpose and Self. These creations will be easily planted and tended clearly and wisely, with joy and love.

You are also able to discern when you are negatively aligned with a creation—You are holding an intention that is not *yet* aligned with your true purpose and Self. These seeds, planted out of fear, confusion and doubt, arise from the unhealed obstacles. That's all. While they are blocking positive creations, they are providing you with the information that parts of your self are still in need of healing.

You Cannot Fail

How wonderful to be *self-aware enough to recognize the difference between creations that are in or out of alignment with your true Self.* Life has become an open practice, an adventure. Therefore, it is impossible to fail. By now, you have the wisdom to know that the objective of the path to remembering the truth of who you are is not to be rid of the obstacles. Whenever you realize that you are negatively aligned with a creation, you can take that as an opportunity to practice even more patience and love.

Nor is the path a demand that you move methodically through the seven phases. *As the gardener of your life,* you have the capacity to tend to all the seeds of your creations with patience, care, and loving awareness.

**You Have Always Been Co-Creating Your Life—
Now You Get To Co-Create It Consciously**

By now, you also know that you have always been co-creating your life. Many people create their lives unconsciously. Because of a lack of awareness, these people often believe they are victims rather than co-creators of their life.

They can become bitter, resigned, hopeless, and stuck in unhealthy patterns because they believe they are powerless to change. They believe that the obstacles are the truth of who they are. Not you!

You have learned that the obstacles between you and the truth are simply misunderstandings. Some of your misunderstandings are the ones you have carried for lifetimes and have brought into this life to heal. Others have been promoted by humanity's collective negative unconscious and passed down through cultures, religions, generations, and families into your very own wounds, stories, belief systems, messages, and thoughts.

How liberating it is to know that the truth of who you are is not bound by humanity's missed creations! The word "sin" originally came from a term used in archery. Sin indicated that the archer had "missed the mark" (or target). Humanity, largely bound by the shadow of unconsciousness, has often missed the mark by misunderstanding the gift of being human. This has led to a misuse of the gift by creating unnecessary suffering and cruelty toward ourselves and others.

It took courage for you to question and challenge the seeming truth of the obstacles. Ultimately, they are not personal. They have been deeply imbedded within humanity for eons.

> *"Who are we without our addictions;*
> *without our media-induced hungers?*
> *So often the voices we hear echoing in our mind*
> *are not our own but that of our influencers."*
> —L.M. Browning, *Seasons of Contemplation:*
> *A Book of Midnight Meditations*

It took courage for you to say, "I believe there is more to me and life than the obstacles." It took a brave heart for you to reach deep within yourself, to inquire, to explore, and to emerge with a greater understanding of the truth of who you are.

Your Courageous Heart Leads You!

Your courage has led you to travel through the phases. This movement initiated an opening and a shift in your relationship to the obstacles. Over time, you have realized that obstacles are not your enemies. Nor are they undesired aspects of yourself that need to be gotten rid of, like the plague. Instead, your search has opened the door to compassion. Just like the wise adult who cares for a child's immaturity and counsels them with loving patience, so can you care for the obstacles when they arise with the same degree of understanding. *How liberating to be able to lend patience and kindness to yourself when you become afraid and reactive.* How freeing to see the obstacles for what they are—misunderstandings—and to be able to tend to them without believing and succumbing to them.

You Can Only Grow

Now, through self-knowledge, you can co-create your life with the understanding that you get to choose! It's your one beautiful, wild life! Since you *cannot* fail, you grow.

You experience the results of your creations and do the work of self inquiry to further clear away your misunderstandings. In this way, *transformation naturally occurs*. This journey brings you into direct experience of the Illuminated being that you are!

2. EXPERIENCING:
The Act of Living Your Creations

Every thought is a creation that yields itself to experience. Every emotion is the direct experience of thought. And every action in your life is a combination of thoughts and feelings. Thus, each day is filled with a lifetime of experiences which you can use to support your awakening. Something as simple as sweeping the floor is guided by your intention behind the act of sweeping and the resulting thoughts and feelings you have about your creation of sweeping.

In 1985, when I was fully awake and Illuminated for one week, I had the realization that I could be blissfully happy washing dishes for the rest of my life. In that moment, I realized that what I am *doing* is not important. How I am with whatever I am doing—that's what's important.

(Pause for a moment to reflect:
What are you doing in this very moment?
Are you immersed in the miracle this moment offers?
Are you present, joyful or perhaps distracted, resentful...?
Whatever your current state, see if just for a moment
you can let yourself drop beneath the surface
of things to experience the river of peace
connecting you and your actions as one.)

Experiencing is creation's partner. The purpose of experiencing is to give you infinite opportunities *to discern your creations,* learning from them. Whether you have missed the mark in a creation or if your aim is true, recognizing the difference through experiencing increases your education of awareness and awakening.

3. PAUSE:
Slow Down, Take Time to Go Inside and Connect with Yourself

In your Living Practice, remember to employ "PAUSE" on a regular basis. It is easy to get caught up in life and forget for a moment or a day or two that THIS IS *your life* you are creating and experiencing. Pausing deepens your ability to be present and in relationship with yourself and all that is. The act of pausing is to intentionally slow down and go inside into the felt sense within your body. When you pause, it is the act of experiencing what you are feeling in your body in this moment. It could be an emotion, a thought, or a physical sensation. *Inside your body is where you experience life*, your creations, and all aspects of consciousness. In other words, experiencing your life is an inside job—it is not happening outside of you.

Here's a very simple example. When you see someone or something you love, you feel this love in the area in your chest. Your heart opens. It is an emotional and physical sensation. When you feel anger toward someone or something, your heart closes. This, too, is an emotional and physical experience. By slowing down and pausing periodically throughout your day (especially when troubled) and by going inside to the felt sense in your body, you will learn to track when you are open/responsive to life and when you are closed/reactive. Cultivating this awareness is essential. Pausing coupled with self inquiry, can help you grow your awareness with what you are experiencing.

4. INQUIRY:
The Process of Self Inquiry Regarding Your Creations and Experiences

You know that *inquiry is one of your most powerful tools for awakening*. Just as judging closes you, inquiry gently opens you.

Creations and experiences can get caught and blocked by the obstacles. Remember, obstacles are historical. They are bound to the past or projected onto an imaginary future, by a limited self-identity. Now that you have the capacity to engage in self inquiry about your creations and experiences, you have the power to bring yourself out of the past or future and back into the moment of NOW. You also get to loosen the constraints of a narrow sense of self and expand your experience of self. This happens quite naturally in the inquiry process.

Here is another example of the self inquiry process/ The WAE-witnessing, asking and experiencing (a previous example was in the Committed Phase): You lie down to sleep. Suddenly, you have a worrisome thought (*the creation*) about an unresolved issue in your life. You pause, go inside, *experiencing* what you feel inside your body and around you. Inside—perhaps your heart is racing, or your thoughts are judging, fearful, repetitive and outside—perhaps the room feels hot or cold. Employing the tool of *self inquiry*, you ask yourself: "What's here now?" Or "What is my unmet need in this moment?" Or "Who is the I that is experiencing?" Or "Who am I?" After asking, you *pause* again to *experience* while *witnessing*, the felt sense in your body *in the moment* as well as what you experience around you. Repeating the question(s) and tracking your experience brings you back into the NOW. It expands your sense of self, connects you to the benevolent observer, Pure Consciousness, the all that is. Inquiry helps you become comfortable in the unknown. Obstacles are based on the known, the familiar. Through this practice of coming back into the NOW and experiencing yourself as a seamless part of all that is, the worrisome future and regretful past cease to exist. The obstacles have lost their tentacled hold on you for the time being. This process, repeated daily, will help you discern the difference between distraction and presence, illusion-wrapped obstacles and truth.

5. TRANSFORMATION:
   Positive Change—It Is Moving from a Lesser to a Higher Place—It Is the Process of Remembering Your Light-Filled, Authentic Self

   After what may have felt like lifetimes of self-betrayal,

hiding behind a mask of pretense, conditioned and trapped by the obstacles, controlled by fear, you are transforming. Your determined work to remember the truth of who you are has wondrous results. *Transformation is not something you do. Transformation is the result of creating, experiencing, pause and inquiry.*

WHEN YOU HAVE YOURSELF, YOU ARE FREE

By doing the work, you are empowered, open, and free. Free to live a purposeful life with loving and compassionate awareness. Accepting the inherent precision of awakening is a wisdom that develops. You come to understand that even after years of dedication to your spiritual journey, doubt and despair can creep in. Life can be turbulent. You accept that there will be moments when you forget the light inside. The wisdom in you through commitment, practice, and knowledge will abide these experiences.

> *"It isn't by getting out of the world*
> *that we become enlightened,*
> *but by getting into the world...*
> *by getting so tuned in*

that we can ride the waves of our existence
and never get tossed
because we become the waves."
—Ken Kesey, *Kesey's Garage Sale*

You have come to understand that every situation comes wrapped as a gift. The gift being that every experience is helping you refine your understanding. It turns the light on in what had previously been darkness. As you let go of misunderstandings, you are lifted higher and higher into the Grace—filled atmosphere of Illumination while deeply grounded in your humanity. From creation to experience to pause to inquiry to transformation, you are finding your way home. Moment by moment. Breath by breath. Heartbeat by heartbeat. Step by step. *The supreme gift of being human is the opportunity to remember the truth of who you are.*

PERCEIVED AS LIGHT
EXPRESSED AS LOVE
EXPERIENCED AS JOY AND PEACE
THIS IS THE TRUTH,
THE TRUTH OF WHO YOU ARE

CHAPTER #12

The Key Points to Embracing the Gift of Being Human

1. Being human is a gift. It is an opportunity to remember the truth of who you are.
2. You are co-creating your life, unconsciously or consciously.
3. You get to experience your creations.
4. Experiencing is creation's partner.
5. Experiencing your life is an inside job.
6. Pause helps you to slow down, go inside, and deepen your ability to be present.
7. Make "PAUSE" one of your favorite mini-practices each day.
8. Self Inquiry (The WAE) is one of your most powerful tools for awakening.
9. Inquiry helps you develop your capacity to be with the unknown and to gently question your limited identity of self.
10. Inquiry helps bring you out of the past or future and back into the present.

11. You get to utilize inquiry as a tool to grow and awaken.
12. Transformation is not something you do.
13. Transformation is the result of creating, experiencing, and inquiry.
14. Transformation is positive change and growth.
15. You have a capacity for self-awareness.
16. With self-awareness you can discern when you are creating out of positive or negative intention.
17. Obstacles are misunderstandings.
18. You have the ability to tend to your misunderstandings with compassion without succumbing to them.
19. You get to learn how to discern and respond to life, rather than project and react.
20. You have freewill.
21. You are responsible for your choices.
22. As co-creator, you are interconnected with all life.
23. Each day is an opportunity to engage life as the Living Practice of creating, experiencing, pause, inquiry, and transformation.
24. Each day is an opportunity to remember the truth of who you are.

THE LIVING PRACTICE #12
Creating, Experiencing, Pause, Inquiry, and Transformation

Find a quiet place for contemplation to consider and write about the following:

1. How do you feel about your gift of being human?

2. When you consider the elements of the Living Practice (create, experience, pause, inquire, transform) which one(s) are you most drawn to and why?

3. Are there any elements of the Living Practice that you are unsure about? Why? (Once you get a sense of what you are unclear about, go back and re-read the sections about the Living Practice).

4. How do you plan to apply the tools you have learned?

5. Going forward, what obstacle calls for your attention and healing?

6. What are the intrinsic qualities about yourself that you have come to recognize? Write down a minimum of three. Carry them with you as reminders of the inherent truth about you.

7. Has your faith evolved? If so, how?

8. From your generous heart, how can you express and share what you received on your path thus far?

Inward journey to Experience the Gift of Being Human
Find a comfortable place to sit or lie down. Close your eyes and focus on your breathing, noticing the state of your breathing... You might discover that your breath is shallow or fast or anxious or deep or quiet. After discovering the quality of your breathing, take three long, slow, deep breaths with the intention to open and relax your body and your mind.... If you are already relaxed, this will support you dropping even deeper into an open state of awareness.

Imagine yourself before incarnating, before being human... You are a spiritual being, sitting high up on a star looking down at the world. Perhaps you have wings that can lift and soar, or perhaps you are a light form that glides swiftly across the galaxy. Whatever spiritual presence you choose to be, you can see into the world and observe people going about their lives... You have been given this opportunity as preparation for your own incarnational human experience.... From this place, you are aware of the light that exists in all of creation.

As you sit, you are fascinated, in wonder, watching people create. There seems to be no limit to what they can create, either positive or negative. They are writing songs, preparing a meal, building bridges, walking their dogs, physically dying, sewing a dress, performing surgery, planning wars, planting gardens, making love, rocking a child, scrounging for food in a trash bin, racing cars, running away, thinking thoughts, shouting, laughing, crying.... everything they do is a creation. From your spiritual perspective, you understand this.

You notice that while creating, some people pause to experience their creations. You also notice that when they do this, their connection to themselves and what they are creating deepens...besides being able to see, you can also hear them. When people pause, you hear many of them asking themselves, "What's here now?" or "What is my unmet need in this moment?" or "Who is the I that is experiencing?" or "Who am I?" When they do this, you notice again that their connection to themselves deepens even more... The more deeply connected they are, the more peaceful they become and the brighter the light inside of them shines... They seem more relaxed with what is, when they pause....

You also notice that many others race around creating, without pausing. They seem to barely breathe. They seem to encounter more difficulty in connecting deeply and in being present in the moment. You notice they tend to be more reactive than the folks who take time in their lives to consciously slow down, experience, pause, and inquire.

As you continue to observe, you see that people who have embraced their human life as a gift tend to be more open and happier, and their lives continue to transform... They seem to be aware that their life is an opportunity to remember the truth of who they are.

Watching all of this, you get excited. You want to go for it! You want to jump into your life and embrace it as a gift. You want to utilize all the tools that you understand are the gifts in being human: The Living Practice, freewill, self-responsibility, self-awareness, natural generosity, connection and love, the human spirit and inspiration and countless opportunities to discern and learn! You turn to Source and ask, "Is it my turn?" You hear a very loving "yes," and within the space of one breath, you are here, right now, in your beautiful human body. Give your self time to experience this transition...Then, with the rest of your beautiful human life before you, you say, "Thank you!"

Gently bringing this inward journey to a close, focus again on your breath. Slowly open your eyes, and when you are ready, sit up... Spend some time writing about your experience of the journey. In particular, you may want to write about what it was like to be the observer and what you felt as you embraced your human life.

An Affirmation of Support for Becoming the Conscious Co-creator of Your Life

"I say yes to life! I say yes to me! I welcome co-creating my life with Spirit. I say thank you to Spirit, God, Source, for this gift of being human, this beautiful opportunity to remember the light inside, my light that shines brightly forever."

*"And I rise to taste the dawn,
and find that love alone will shine today.
And the shining says: to love it all,
and love it madly, and always endlessly,
and ever fiercely, to love without choice
and thus enter the all,
to love it mindlessly and thus be the all,
embracing the only radiant divine:
now as emptiness, now as form,
together and forever,
the godless search undone,
and love alone will shine today."*

—KEN WILBER,
*The Essential Ken Wilber:
An Introductory Reader*

Acknowledgements

Thank you, God/Source/Spirit, for EVERYTHING. My life is yours.

To my Mom whose grace taught me the power of unconditional love. To my Dad for showing me that life is filled with adventure, and that the next great one is right around the corner. To my lifelong companions and teachers—my brothers and sisters (both by blood and by marriage), for believing in me all along the way. To my nieces and nephews, whom I love as fiercely as if they were my own. To John Brown, who taught me that love can be both passionate and kind. To Patti Orrison Davis, my teenage best friend, who invited me to sit with her on the bus when no one else would and said, "I'll be your friend." To Sherry Pae, my grown-up best friend, who is kindness personified. To Gretchen, a living Bodhisattva, and finally, to my spiritual teachers, mentors, and therapists: Swami Muktananda, Amen, Dr. Barbara Brennan, Emilie Conrad, Reverend Rosalyn Bruyere, Dr. Anne Marie Zwycewicz, Dr. John Pierrakos, Dr. Martha Harrell, Bette Barto, Ginny Breckenridge. Thank you for your generous teachings and wise counsel.

Many thanks to my beta readers—Melodie Adinolfi, Phyllis Batezel, Elizabeth Wegoye, Quincy Gilbert and Gretchen Seibert. Your willingness to read the first draft and offer honest feedback was invaluable.

I would also like to thank my writing coach, David Hazard, whose comment, "You are on to something, keep going" was just what I needed to hear when the small voice of self-doubt crept in.

About The Author

At a very young age, Laurie's compassion for all life and a statement made to her Mother that she intended to adopt children from all over the world led her Mother to say, "You are from a different star." As she grew, Laurie's search for answers to the big questions such as, "Who am I? Why are we here? What is the purpose of a human life?" and her passion to explore life's other mysteries intuitively guided her.

In addition to her passion, Laurie's quest for understanding was fueled by a sadness she experienced within herself and witnessed in others when feeling disconnected. She saw how separation led people to feeling lost, without purpose, or to cruel and dismissive acts. A fortuitous invitation to have dinner with the eminent British philosopher Alan Watts in the spring of 1973, confirmed Laurie's belief that spiritual wisdom is possible if one is willing to risk convention in search of truth. A life-threatening illness followed in her mid-twenties. That experience catapulted Laurie on to her own life-saving path and in doing so, she left the world of convention to study healing, spirituality and the evolution of human consciousness with pioneers such as Dr. Barbara Brennan, Reverend Rosalyn Bruyere, Dr. John Pierrakos and Emilie Conrad.

Her multiple trainings led to certifications as a Brennan Healing Science Teacher, Brennan Healing Science Practitioner, Brennan Integration Practitioner, Core Energetic Therapist and Continuum Teacher. Along the way, she studied with White House Pastry Chef, Roland Mesnier, and earned a Bachelor's Degree with an emphasis in comparative literature. Laurie was School Dean of the Barbara Brennan School of Healing (BBSH) and the Barbara Brennan School of Healing Europe (BBSHE), working side by side with Barbara Brennan from 1993-2016. After a two-year hiatus, she returned to BBSH in 2018 as an advisory board member and dean. Laurie also continues her vocation as a spiritual channel, writer, therapist, inspirational speaker and healer, offering teachings and guidance— utilizing her decades of work with energy and consciousness and personal transformation.

Though Laurie never adopted children nor had any of her own, her adult students from over forty countries fulfilled her soul's intention in a unique way—voiced through her as a young child. Her passion was and remains to be, to support people on their spiritual journey home to the truth of who they are. When asked by one of her students why she loves teaching, Laurie had this to say, "The best feeling in the world for me is when a person reclaims another part of their self and they are forever transformed. That is the gold!" When not traveling, lecturing or teaching Laurie lives joyfully in New Jersey.

You can contact Laurie through her website www.lauriekeene.com or via her email info@lauriekeene.com

Made in the USA
Middletown, DE
14 September 2020